$6.95 Paper Back
$8.95 Library Binding

SINCERE'S
BICYCLE
Service BOOK

by
WILLIAM EWERS

PUBLISHED BY
SINCERE PRESS
POST OFFICE BOX 10422
PHOENIX, ARIZONA 85016

First Printing -October 1970
Second Printing-September 1971

LC Number 72-20654
SBN 0-912534-02-8

Introduction.

This book was written for kids of all ages. With increased emphasis on exercise for health in our affluent society, more oldsters are taking to the road than ever before. Bicycles built with stationary stands for exercise, and three wheelers for our senior citizens, are now commonplace.

Bicycles have been the principal mode of transportation in most of the World since the late 1890's. The automobile came to the United States about the same time, easing the bike out as an item of necessity. With the possible exception of the paper route standby, it has been used mostly for pleasure.

I hope this book will make it easier for kids, and their long suffering old dads, to service and repair their machines. Most bikes today are made in Europe, or Japan, and imported into the country. Many makes use same parts and service procedures, making it easy for the novice mechanic.

Remember, your bicycle is a precision machine. Treat it with respect and regular maintenance care.

Happy cycling.

William Ewers

Other books by Sincere Press:

Sincere's Sewing Machine Service Book, 2nd Ed. William Ewers
Sincere's History of the Sewing Machine, W. Ewers & H. W. Baylor
Sincere's Zig Zag Sewing Machine Service Book, William Ewers
Sincere's Mini-Bike Service Book, William Ewers & Irv Charles
Sincere's Lawn Mower Service Book, William Ewers

Chapter One

History.

The forerunner of our present-day bicycle was invented sometime a-round 1790, by a Frenchman named de Sivrac. His machine was a simple mechanism which he propelled by moving his feet along the ground. He mounted it near the rear wheel, and after running briskly for a few yards, would lift his feet and ride. The machine had one big drawback. It was impossible to steer any direction but straight ahead since inventor de Sivrac hadn't found a way to turn the front wheel. What he lacked in ingenuity he made up for in design as his machines bore the likeness of several different animals.

The machine didn't attract much attention until the German inventor Karl Drais produced his improved version in 1816. Baron Drais' bicycle was called the Draisine. It's prominent feature was a wooden steering bar attached to the front wheel. The seat was a formed wooden saddle mounted on a horizontal bar, and together with two forks for the wheels, made up the main frame.

Needless to say, after the Draisine became popular, France insisted inventor de Sivrac recieve full credit for the invention since the German cycle was obviously a copy. Nothing much was resolved.

There are still a few Draisine machines in various museums around the world.

Figure One

The first workable bicycle with pedals was invented in 1860, by another Frenchman, a locksmith named Ernest Michaux. His prototype featured a front wheel with pedals. Before that time a few bikes with pedals had appeared in England, but Michaux's was the first successful model.

There was even controversy over the invention in Michaux's own shop. One of his workers named Pierre Lallemont claimed he was the actual inventor of the two pedal concept, which he discovered when he reversed the wheels on a perambulator. Lallemont finally left France and later turned up in the United States where he was granted a patent, in 1860, for a crank-driven velocipede.

During the period from 1850 to 1900, hundreds of different vehicles appeared, both in the United States and Europe. They ranged from gear-driven chairs on wheels, to all shapes and sizes of tricycles. Some were hand-driven. Others employed the foot pedal principal.

The coaster brake, chain drive, and handle bar, as we know them today, first appeared in the late 1880's. Roller bearings were used initially in the 1870's.

Bike riders first called their machine a bicycle in 1869. High-Wheelers were in vogue at the time and enjoyed popularity for decades. The front wheel was almost as tall as a man, and the rear wheel was much smaller. It required a real sense of balance to stay mounted on a high-wheeler. Several of these machines are still around and can be seen in parades, circus, and comedy acts.

Figure Two

A typical High-Wheeler.

The bicycle as we know it today first appeared in 1880. Both wheels were the same size and the sprocket with chain drive was quite common. Wheels contained rubber tires and the traditional frame shape was in style. Women type frames also were manufactured during this era.

The saddle seat, formed handle bars, spokes, pedals and fenders were added, or improved, as riders became more safety minded.

Balloon tires were first utilized in 1889, but were't really safe or pract - ical until cord-reinforcing construction was first used in 1895. By early 1900 the racing element discovered the cycle, and bike riding reached a pinnacle of sorts.

Racing bikes became a big thing and the sport was extremely popular during the 1900's. Bike racing is still a big sport but will never reach the popularity of that golden era when Mile-a-Minute Murphy was the most famous bicycle racer in the World. His name was a household word in 1900.

The racing bike hasn't changed much. All unnecessary equipment is still stripped from the machine to make it as light as possible.

Figure Three

Sleek racing bicycle-Made in Japan.

Bike riding is becoming more than a hobby in America as more and more people return to the bike's functional uses. Air polution and bad health as bad omens have turned thousands back to the two-wheeler. A recent concept of adding a third wheel, making the unit into an oversized tricycle, has caught on with the over-fifty set. Many bicycle plants specialize in building conversion kits.

Together with the motor bike, the bicycle is gaining widespread use. Bike sales have soared and there's nothing to indicate that it's just a passing fad.

The bicycle industry in Japan and Europe have found a new choice plum for their wares, as barriers of prejudice against buying foreign-made merchandise has all but dropped from the American scene. Domestic makers have also experienced new growth.

Bicycle riding is here to stay.

The Unicycle.

The Three-Wheeler

The bicycle industry in Japan.

A front fork brazing machine.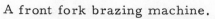

An automatic spoke machine.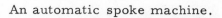

A final assembly line in one of Japan's largest bicycle factories.

Chapter Two

How to assemble your bike:

There are almost as many ways to assemble your bike as there are bikes. Some are right, some are wrong. This chapter illustrates one easy method.

Figure one illustrates several sub-assemblies with the corresponding number indicating order of assembly on the frame.

If your bike is new, remove all parts from the shipping carton and put them in order on the floor. If you're merely adding one particular part or sub-assembly such as a wheel or axle, refer to that phase of assembly.

Figure One

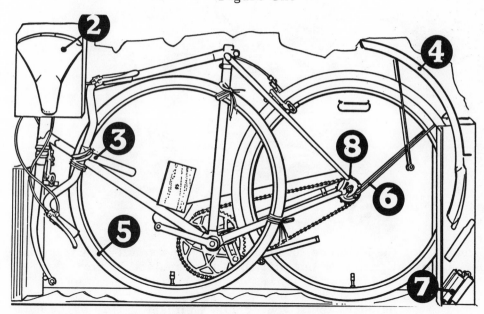

Figure 2, overpage, illustrates the saddle(or seat).
1. Fit the seat post to the seat(if not already unitized).
2. Tighten seat nut(B).
3. Adjust to required height.
      a. A good rule for proper seat placement is: The riders toe should touch the ground, but the heel shouldn't. Many riders prefer a high seat, but the knee should still bend slightly when pedaling.
4. Tighten seat bolt nut(A). Most manufacturers suggest at least 2 1/2" of the seat post should remain in the frame.

Since bikes are made in many different countries, nuts and bolt sizes do vary slightly. In most cases 1/2" or 9/16" open wrench should do the job. If the bike has several different size bolts, use a crescent wrench.

Figure Two

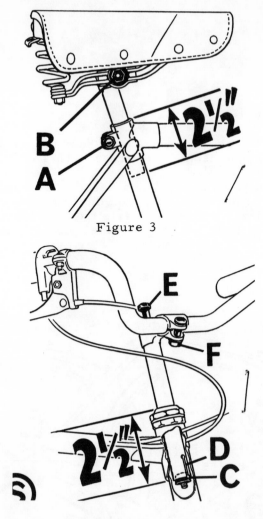

Figure 3

When putting the handlebar in place be sure the small lug(C), on the expander cone is aligned with one slot(D) in the handlebar stem.

1. Leave expander bolt(E) loose.
2. Fit handlebar into frame head.
3. Adjust handlebars to fit your grip. At least 2 1/2" of the handlebars remain in steering column frame. When adjusting handlebar, do so at point(F).
4. Tighten expander bolt(E), using a 1/2" or 9/16" wrench.
5. Adjust handle grips to desired angle.
6. Tighten handlebar stem nut(F). The stem is also known as a gooseneck. Proper installation finds the neck facing away from the rider.
7. Re-check handlebar adjusting nut(F). For complete safety, handlebars must be held firmly in place.
8. Use rubber grips for hands whenever possible.
9. Your comfort is important. Adjust handlebars to you.
   a. When adding high-rise unit, tighten holding bolt firmly.
   b. Racing style handlebars should also be chosen for comfort.

Figure 4

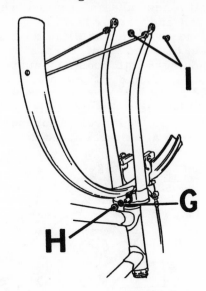

After attaching the handlebar, turn the bike upside down and put fender in place between front forks.

1. To avoid scratching your bike, put it on an old blanket or sheet.
2. Remove nut(H), and washer(G), figure 4.
3. Slide fender between fork blades. Fork blades must face forward.
   a. Angle fender slightly to fit between forks. Don't bend fender.
4. If bike is equipped with caliper brakes, fit fender tab over bolts.
5. Replace washer(G), and nut(H), and hand tighten.
6. Place fender braces in place over axle(I).
7. Slip washers on axle and hand tighten nuts on both sides.
8. Align the fender and tighten nuts securely.
   a. Use a 1/2" or 9/16" wrench.

Figure 5

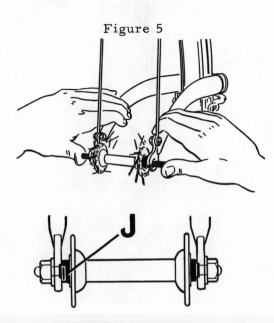

Figure 5, page 11 illustrates proper way to install the front wheel. Remove wooden blocks if a new bike and remove wheel from shipping carton.

1. Remove nut, bolt and washer from both sides of the front axle (if you haven't already done so when installing the front fender.
2. Place the wheel between front forks.
3. Place cone shoulders into round openings on fork ends.
4. Adjusting cone (J) should fit into place on the left side (from riding position).
5. Align the wheel before tightening axle nuts firmly.
6. Turn bike upright and re-check for proper alignment. If there's too much play in the wheel at axle point, adjust the cone (J) inward until it's corrected.

Figure 6

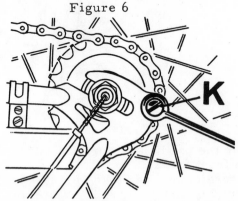

To fit rear fender in place, remove bolts, washers and nuts from the frame ends.

1. Assemble bolt (K) through washer, and fender brace end.
2. Screw bolt (K) into frame end and tighten from inside of locknut.

Figure 7

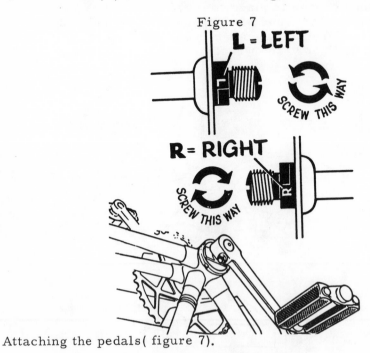

Attaching the pedals (figure 7).

1. Fit pedal with(R) imprint on axle, to chainwheel hanger.
   a. Turn axle clockwise and tighten.
2. Fit pedal with(L) imprint on axle end, to left hanger.
   a. Turn counterclockwise and tighten.

Figure 8

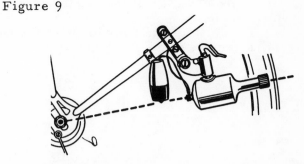

Fig.A **Fig.B**

If your bike comes equipped with the Sturmey Archer 3 speed gear, the rear axle assembly will be set up as follows:
1. Loosen adjuster(1) and disconnect gear control cable.
2. Screw chain guide(3) in against axle nut(4), finger tight.
3. Re-connect control guide.
4. To adjust hub gear, place trigger control lever, or twist control if your bike is so equipped, in middle gear position.
5. Tighten locknut(2).
6. Observe chain through small window in chain guide(figure B).
7. Screw cable adjuster(1), down until the last link in the chain clears the axle.
8. Adjust cable until end of rod is exactly even with the outside end of the axle(see figure B).
9. Tighten locknut(2) firmly to cable adjuster(1).
   a. The above adjustment should work for all three gears.

Figure 9

If your bike is equipped with tire-driven dynamo, fit it and the taillight to left backbrace(figure 9).
1. Fit headlight to front fork with a bracket(generally furnished).
2. If battery operated light is used, attach to front fork stem.

When you've completely assembled the bike, re-check all sub-assemblies for proper adjustment.

Steering head adjustment is illustrated in figure 10.

Figure 10

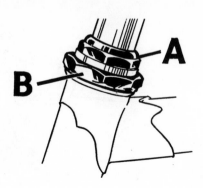

The steering mechanism should be free of drag, or play, in the head bearings. If the head requires adjustment, especially after bike is ridden over rough ground, refer to adjustment text below.

1. If adjustment to head is required, loosen locknut(A), figure 10.
2. Tighten headnut (B) gently, until steering head turns freely without excess play.
3. Tighten locknut(A).

Handlebar adjustment is very important and goes hand-in-glove with the steering assembly. The handlebars should be adjusted so your arms are always in a relaxed position, not too close to the body, and not extended too far away from the body.

To lower or raise the handlebars;

1. Loosen expander bolt(A), two full turns and give it a gentle tap to release the expander cone, which allows the stem to move.
2. Adjust handlebar to suit you, and tighten the bolt(X).
3. At least 2 1/2" of the handlebar stem MUST remain in the steering fork frame.
4. To adjust up and down angle of the handlebars, loosen nut(Y), figure 11, and move to the desired angle. Tighten locknut(Y).

Figure 11

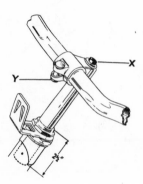

If your bike is equipped with a front wheel brake, adjust as follows;
1.   Loosen knurled locknut(A), figure 12.
2.   Turn adjuster screw (B), counterclockwise, until set blocks barely clear the wheel rim.
3.   Tighten locknut(A), while holding unit firmly in place.
4.   If one block is closer to the wheel than the other, tap the opposite coil of spring at point(D).
5.   Check nuts(E), they must be tight.
6.   Closed end of brake block holder must face front of bike.
7.   If blocks are worn, or cables frayed, replace them at once.

Figure 12

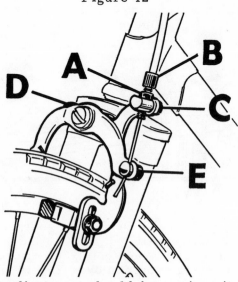

Pedals and pedal adjustment should be a minor item if both pedals are properly installed. Pedal marked (R) on the right hanger, pedal marked (L), on the left hanger.
   1.   If the pedal crank turns hard, adjust lockring(A), using a punch and hammer. Place punch in a notch and tap counterclockwise as needed.
   2.   Turn cup(B) until it's tight. Turn back slightly and tighten ring(A). Some bikes have the simple crank as one piece, others utilize the individual hanger system.
   1.   To remove hanger style, drive cotter pin out. See figure 13A.

Figure 13

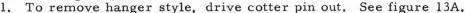

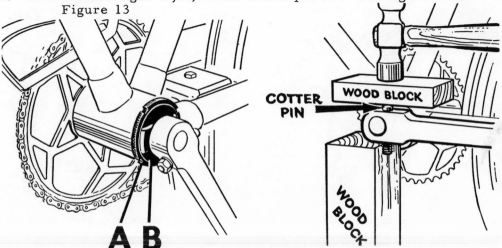

Chain adjustment is very important to good bike operation. A well adjusted chain should have about 1/2" play(up and down measurement) midway between the chainwheel and sprocket. See figure 14.

1. To adjust chain tension, loosen axle nuts(A) figure 14, and move the wheel until proper adjustment is attained.

2. Re-center the wheel in the frame and tighten axle nuts(A).

3. If gear control needs re-adjusting after chain adjustment, refer to figure 15, if bike has Derailleur system. For Sturmey Archer gear, refer to page 13.

4. If chain was removed, replace with connecting link clip with closed end facing direction of chain movement(insert C, figure 14).

    a. Figure 14 is illustrated with bike in upside down position, which is proper position for making the chain adjustment.

Figure 14

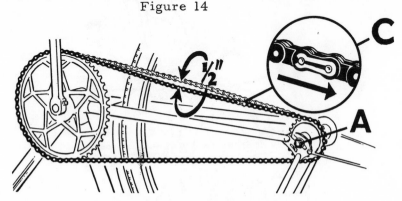

If your bike is equipped with a Derailleur gear, realign the chain per instructions illustrated in figure 15.

1. To adjust the control (10 speed only), turn screw(A) figure 15A, to move the cage to a central position over EACH chainwheel, when the control is in a relative position.

2. Move chain to small freewheel sprocket and adjust outward movement of gear mechanism with screw(A), figure 15.

3. Inward movement of the gear mechanism is adjusted with stop screw (B), to prevent chain from riding over large freewheel sprocket into the spokes.

4. To regulate chain tension, place terminal spring loop(C) into one of the four tension slots in the outer cage plate.

Figure 15   Figure 15A

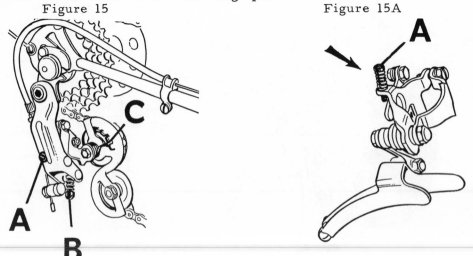

Hub adjustment, front and rear, is important. All wheel nuts must be tight at all times. Loose axle nuts cause worn bearings. If excessive play is present at wheel rim, and wheel nuts are tight, adjust the hub cone.

1. Loosen wheel nuts and cone locknut. Tighten adjusting cone on the side with flat surface to accept a wrench. DO NOT touch the other cone with a wrench or pliers.

2. When properly adjusted, there will be no play at the hub, and only slight play at the wheel rim.

3. Tighten the locknut.

4. If repeated adjustment fails to correct the problem, replace cones since they're probably worn beyond repair.

Figure 16

Basic tools needed for good bike service and repair. Most are readily available from your local bike dealer, or a auto parts store.

Figure 17

DUMBELL SPANNER

A selection of specialty tools:

Figure 18

PEDAL-SPANNERS

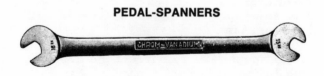

Chapter Three

The Wheel and related components.

The bicycle wheel is made up of several components. The rim, spokes, axle assembly, tire and tube, form the wheel assembly. High speed axles, multiple gears and coaster brakes are also related and will be covered in a later chapter.

Figure 19

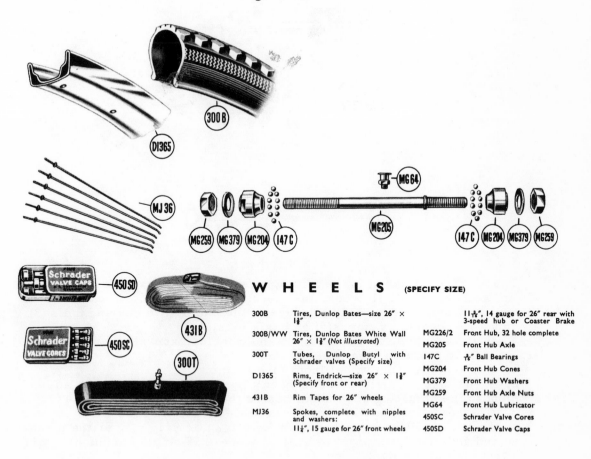

W H E E L S (SPECIFY SIZE)

300B	Tires, Dunlop Bates—size 26″ × 1⅜″	
300B/WW	Tires, Dunlop Bates White Wall 26″ × 1⅜″ (Not illustrated)	
300T	Tubes, Dunlop Butyl with Schrader valves (Specify size)	
D1365	Rims, Endrick—size 26″ × 1⅜″ (Specify front or rear)	
431B	Rim Tapes for 26″ wheels	
MJ36	Spokes, complete with nipples and washers: 11¼″, 15 gauge for 26″ front wheels 11 7/16″, 14 gauge for 26″ rear with 3-speed hub or Coaster Brake	
MG226/2	Front Hub, 32 hole complete	
MG205	Front Hub Axle	
147C	7/32″ Ball Bearings	
MG204	Front Hub Cones	
MG379	Front Hub Washers	
MG259	Front Hub Axle Nuts	
MG64	Front Hub Lubricator	
450SC	Schrader Valve Cores	
450SD	Schrader Valve Caps	

The Front Wheel.

The front wheel fits in place between the front forks. It turns on a cone and bearing arrangement contained in the hub. Front cone assemblies vary from maker to maker but basic service procedures should apply to most units. If you have a different assembly not covered by this text, write directly to the manufacturer of the bike.

Figure 20 illustrates components in a typical front axle assembly.

Figure 20

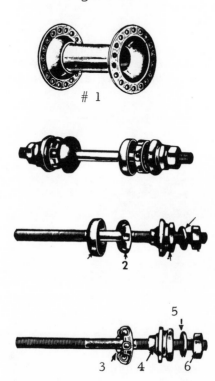

1

2

5

3   4   6

The hub(1) is attached to the rim by a series of spokes, normally thirty six in number, and it also contains the axle components. The axle (2) is threaded on each end and held in place in the hub by two bearing units (3), an adjusting cone(4), washers(5) and axle nuts(6).

When the front wheel works loose and wobbles excessively at the rim, adjustment is made on front wheel cone.

1. Remove the front wheel from bike frame.
2. If the bike is fairly new and hasn't been abused, the simple adjustment to the adjusting cone should solve the problem.
3. The adjusting cone is smooth on one end and notched for a wrench on the other. Place wrench, generally a 1/2" or 9/16", over the notched end and turn clockwise(inward) until there is no play at the hub, and slight play at the rim.
4. Replace the wheel. Center wheel in forks before tightening nuts.
5. If the bike is old and repeated adjustment doesn't correct the problem, replace both bearings and the adjusting cone.

6. To replace the bearings, follow preceding steps and turn adjusting cone completely off the axle. Replace bearings with the same brand as your old set. Most bearing assemblies ARE NOT interchangeable.
    a. When replacing bearing units remember: The bevel side of the unit always faces inward toward the hub.
7. Lubricate the bearings with grease and clean hub area before replacing the assembly.
8. If the adjusting cone and bearings wear out frequently, check your hub. If it is cracked, bent or broken, replace at once.
9. If the wheel suddenly locks, check axle nuts. You've probably been riding your bike with loose nuts. If locking nut keeps working loose, add another nut to each end. The second nut acts as a locknut.
    a. After tightening nuts, recheck the wheel. It must move freely without binding. If there's some binding, recheck the cone setting. If set too close, back it off slightly.
    b. Never hold the axle, or any threaded part on your bike, with a pair of pliers or other tool which could damage the threads.

The Rear Wheel.

When removing the rear wheel for service, turn your bike upside down, for easier access to parts and sub-assemblies.
1. Remove the chain by slipping it off the crank sprocket.
2. Loosen rear axle nuts.
3. If the bike is equipped with a coaster brake, remove the brake arm clip.
4. Pull fender braces aside and remove the wheel.
5. If the bike is equipped with a 3, 5, or 10 speed axle or gear set-up, refer to the chapter covering the unit for removal instructions.
6. To install rear wheel after service, simply reverse removal steps after checking the adjusting cone and wheel for proper bearing alignment. The wheel must be able to turn freely.
    a. Replace the chain over rear sprocket and replace wheel in the frame.
    b. Put on a washer, the fender brace, another washer, and finally the axle nut.
    c. Replace the brake clip on models with a coaster brake.
    d. Start chain moving into place by placing a few links on the crank sprocket and turning pedals toward rear of the bike. Chain should track into place without any trouble.
    e. Tighten rear axle nuts after centering the wheel, and checking the chain for proper amount of play(1/2" at center of chain).
    f. Re-check brake adjustment.
    g. Tighten axle nuts completely, and spin the wheel. If the wheel appears sluggish, re-adjust the cone.
    h. If there's a grating or rattling sound the cones may be loose.
    i. Always adjust notched cone. It's on the sprocket side of rear axle.
    j. Check rear axle frequently. A loose axle will cause trouble.
    k. If the axle has enough thread use the two locknut system.
    l. There is a commercial product available that will also hold the nut firmly in place, yet will release easily when needed.

The Spoke.

The standard 26" wheeled rim contains 36 spokes. The spokes connect the hub with the rim, and any loose or damaged, can throw the hub out of line, causing severe damage to bearings, axle, rim, tire and finally, to the entire bicycle.

Spoke replacement isn't complicated if basic instructions are closely followed. Spokes cross each other and nearby spokes must be moved when replacing neighboring units. Use a spoke wrench whenever possible.

To tighten loose spokes, remove tire, tube and liner from the rim. It's easiest to start at the spoke nearest the valve hole and continue, clockwise, around the rim. After every spoke has been tightened, check the wheel.

If the wheel is straight and true, tighten each spoke at least one, preferably two complete turns. Replace all bent or broken spokes, replace the tire, tube and liner. Replace the wheel in forks.

If the wheel has been damaged by running into a curb, or equally hard object, and has a flat spot as a result, replace the rim. When replacing the rim it's necessary to re-spoke the entire wheel.

Figure 21

Spokes, a section of rim, and a typical spoke wrench.

 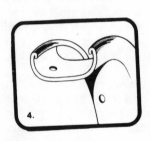 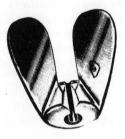

Before spoking the entire wheel, notice the hole configuration in the rim and location of holes in each flange of the hub. The standard 26" rim has a series of 36 holes staggered around the rim. As spokes are installed, the sequence is formed so they cross. The crossing adds strength and rigidity to the wheel. Holes in the flanges do not face opposite, but are off-set slightly from each other.

Figure 22   Figure 22A

To spoke the entire wheel, first place a spoke through both hub flanges, and center them at a slight angle, figure 22A. The first spoke is used to guide additional spokes to proper position.

1.   Place the second spoke in first hole left of guiding spoke of hub, and first hole to the right of valve hole in the rim.

2.   Place the following spoke through the same side of hub flange to left of first spoke placed. Fasten this spoke in 14th rim hole used for down-spoke.

3.   Turn the wheel over and repeat above steps with two spokes.

4.   Place the next spoke up through hub flange in the first hole to right of guiding spoke, and fasten in rim hole to the right of valve hole.

5.   The next spoke is a down spoke from rim down through hub flange in hole to the right of previous spoke placement.   Fasten this spoke in fourteenth rim hole to left of rim hole for previous spoke.

6.   Continue placing spokes around the wheel.   Every other one should be an UP spoke.   Every other spoke should be a DOWN spoke.

7.   Check spoke placement.   If complete, turn wheel over.

    a.   Every other hole in the hub flange should be filled with a spoke head. and all rim holes on the wheel should be filled and two holes on opposite row should be filled with first two installed.

8.   When all spokes are in place, tighten each nipple until threads are completely covered. Check the wheel and if it appears straight and true, tighten each spoke two turns, beginning at the valve hole.

9.   File away all uneven spokes protruding through the rim.

These instructions are for the standard 26" rim.   For 24" rim with 28 spokes, use the 10th hole instead of 14(skip nine holes).   For the 20" rim with fewer spokes, use the 8th hole(skip seven holes).

Spokes are pretty standard, but always tell your dealer the correct size wheel so he can furnish the proper spoke.

REMEMBER: Spoke placement follows a pattern.   One goes up through the hub flange, the next comes down.

Figure 23   Figure 24

Bicycle tires are similiar to automobile tires and are available in a variety of sizes, grades and purposes. Racing tires are different than touring tires. A different grade tire is required for the country bike rider with, poor roads and rough terrain with thickets, than the city rider whose only problem is finding uncrowded pavement to travel. The same holds true for tubes.

Figure 25 illustrates different grade tires available to the bike rider.

Figure 25

Bicycle tires and tubes are graded, just like automobile tires. Cheap tires won't last nearly as long as more expensive tires. They have less tread and the carcass isn't as well built. If you have a need for good tires because of your job, or the terrain you travel, always buy the better tire. A few cents difference should bring many additional hours of wear. Name brand tires similiar to those pictured on page 24 are always a good buy.

The tire should always be inflated properly. If you didn't recieve the pressure chart with your bike, check with your dealer for proper pressure. Some balloon tires require less pressure than others.

The chart on page 26 is distributed by Dunlop(European tire maker) for use on their equipment, but it can be used as a general guide.

A good rule of thumb is the weight factor. If more weight is added to the bike, add more air. Use caution and don't over-inflate. Too much air may be as harmful as too little.

Figure 26 illustrates two major causes of tire failure. The first was damaged by over-inflation. Use an air guage if possible. If a guage isn't available, press your fingers against the tire and if it's firm to the touch, you probably have enough air.

The second illustration shows damage from improper mounting. The size MUST match the rim size exactly. Don't try forcing a too small tire on a rim.

Figure 26

If a tire constantly loses air, it probably needs attention.
1. Place the tire into a tub of water. If the water bubbles, locate the source of trouble, mark it, and remove tire from the water.
2. If source of bubbles is the valve stem area, check it.
3. Remove valve cap and drop water on the stem opening. If it bubbles the valve stem is either loose, or weak.
    a. If loose, reverse the valve cap(figure 28a #8331), and screw it down on valve stem as needed.
    b. If leak doesn't stop, remove the core (8332) and replace with a new one. A new core should be available from any parts store.
4. If the leak persists, check entire valve stem area. The stem may have pulled away from the tube. Turn to following page and follow steps to repair as needed.

Figure 27

5.   When the tube is damaged beyond repair, replace with a new one and keep old one for patches and a spare valve stem.

Figure 28

Valve Assembly-American Pattern   Valve Assembly-European Pattern

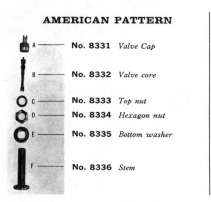

AMERICAN PATTERN

A —— No. 8331 *Valve Cap*

B —— No. 8332 *Valve core*

C —— No. 8333 *Top nut*

D —— No. 8334 *Hexagon nut*

E —— No. 8335 *Bottom washer*

F —— No. 8336 *Stem*

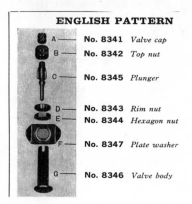

ENGLISH PATTERN

A —— No. 8341 *Valve cap*

B —— No. 8342 *Top nut*

C —— No. 8345 *Plunger*

D —— No. 8343 *Rim nut*

E —— No. 8344 *Hexagon nut*

F —— No. 8347 *Plate washer*

G —— No. 8346 *Valve body*

6.   If entire valve assembly is damaged, cut around old part and remove. Replace with a new part.
      a.   Apply in same manner as a patch.   Clean the tube thoroughly, apply adhesive, and place valve assembly over hole cut in the tube.
7.   If tube is punctured, first try a good puncture sealant. PUNCTURE SEAL is a good brand.   If hole is too large, patch it.
8.   The best bet is a patch kit sold by "CAMEL", or "MONKEY GRIP". Both are available in most parts stores, or auto parts stores.   They are available in round, diamond or oblong shapes.
9.   To repair, remove the tube from rim.   Use caution and don't use a sharp tool which might permanently damage the tire and tube.
      a.   Inflate the tube and repeat water test, dunking it to determine location of puncture.
      b.   When you find the spot, release the air and rough the spot with scraper from the repair kit.
      c.   Follow instructions on the repair kit.   Apply glue, remove the protective cover from the patch and place patch over puncture.
      d.   Allow glue to dry for a few minutes before replacing tube in tire and repeat the dunking to insure patch is secure.
      e.   Replace tube in tire and place them on the rim.
      f.   Inflate to proper pressure.
      g.   Be sure valve stem is placed straight up and down in hole.   If it is set in at an angle, damage will result.
      Removal and replacement of the tire and tube are critical chores and must be performed carefully.
1.   If tire isn't completely flat, loosen valve core and force air out.
2.   Remove one section, of one side of tire.   Use small tire iron, or a wide-head screwdriver.   CAUTION: Don't pinch tire bead.
3.   After one side is started, remove tire all around and slip tube out.
4.   Slip other side of tire away from rim.   Unless tire is damaged, its not necessary to remove it completely.
      a.   If puncture was made by a large object, remove the foreign matter.   If hole is too large (other than nail or wire puncture), patch it in a similiar method as tube patching.   If hole is large, use a boot.

When replacing the tube in a tire and placing them on the rim, inflate the tube slightly and hold valve stem.

1. Position tire on the rim with valve stem near valve hole.
2. Work bead of tire over rim on one side. Use hands only. A tool might damage the tire bead, or the tube.
3. Position valve stem until it's perfectly straight in valve stem hole.
4. Work the other side of tire onto rim by hand. If it's too difficult, let air out of the tube, but don't use a tool if you can avoid it.
5. Work entire tire onto rim and inflate again. After it's been formed in place around the rim, inflate to proper pressure.

Good tire care is very important. If you notice excessive wear on the rear tire, rotate it to the front, and bring the front tire back.

NEVER OPERATE YOUR BIKE ON A LOW TIRE:

Figure 29
Tire pressure chart by Dunlop Tire Company.

DUNLOP		Weight of rider			
		125 lb.	150 lb.	175 lb.	200 lb.
TOURIST SPRITE (White Sidewall)	1¼"	45 lb.	54 lb.	60 lb.	65 lb.
ROADSTER, SPORTS (except 27×1¼),	1⅜"	43 lb.	50 lb.	55 lb.	60 lb.
WHITE ROADSTER (White Sidewall),	1¼"	38 lb.	45 lb.	50 lb.	55 lb.
CHAMPION, CARRIER, BATES	1⅜"	33 lb.	40 lb.	45 lb.	50 lb.
TANDEM	1⅜"	38 lb.	45 lb.	50 lb.	55 lb.
SPEED (White Sidewall), WHITE SPRITE	1¼"	65 lb.	70 lb.	75 lb.	80 lb.
(White Sidewall), SPRITE (Amber Sidewall),	1⅜"	60 lb.	65 lb.	70 lb.	75 lb.
SPORTS 27×1¼)					
ROAD RACING (High Pressure) 1¼" Road Work		70 lb.	80 lb.	85 lb.	90 lb.
Track Work		80 lb.	90 lb.	95 lb.	100 lb.

Chapter Four

The Frame, Fork, and Handlebars.

The frame of the bicycle is like the body of a car. It has no working parts, yet all working parts are dependent on it. The front fork and handlebar assembly pass through the front opening. The crank passes through the lower center frame, and the seat is attached to the upper area. The rear axle, wheel assembly fits into two notches on the lower rear of the frame, and all attachments are fastened to it in some manner.

Unless the bike has been wrecked or mistreated, service to the frame itself should be almost nil.

However, if the bike has been damaged and the frame is out of line, causing the chain to track improperly, adjustment isn't too much of a problem.

1. Remove both wheels, crank, and front fork if necessary.

2. Place the frame in a bench vise and clamp tightly.

3. Apply pressure to frame in proper direction to straighten. Continue until frame is perfectly straight.

4. If the frame breaks, have it welded at your local welding shop.

5. After service, check for proper alignment by placing the frame on a table. Place a straight edge along the body. If there's no gap, the frame is true. If there's a gap under the straight edge, straighten frame at that spot.

After a bike is ridden for some time, the rear axle retaining gaps have a tendency to spread, allowing too much play in rear axle assembly. If it isn't corrected, permanent damage may result, especially if you have a multi-gear axle.

To correct, remove the rear wheel and place rear forks in a vise, one at a time, and press together as needed. If a vise isn't available, make a stopgap repair by placing a pair of washers on each side of both forks, on the axle.

Figure 30

The Seat.

The bicycle seat is probably completely overlooked when the buyer is looking for useable features. However, size and conformity are very important to good comfort.

A quality seat, with sound seat construction and top grade covering, should be the goal for every bike owner. Racing seats are another thing and should be chosen for reasons other than comfort.

For easy cycling, the seat should be positioned so the rider can touch ground with his toe, but not his heel. When the foot is on the down pedal the knee should bend slightly.

Seats are attached to the seat post in a variety of ways. Most seat posts are adjustable up and down. Some are adjustable back and forth.

Figure 31 illustrates different style seats and sub-assembly components.

The seat post is generally adjustable, but at least 2 1/2" of the post should remain in the frame, for complete safety.

There are two different style seat clamps.
1. The first is the swivel style. It's possible to adjust seat tilt.
2. The second is attached to the spring seat and may be moved along the spring. To tilt the seat up and down, loosen the adjusting screw & move the seat as needed.

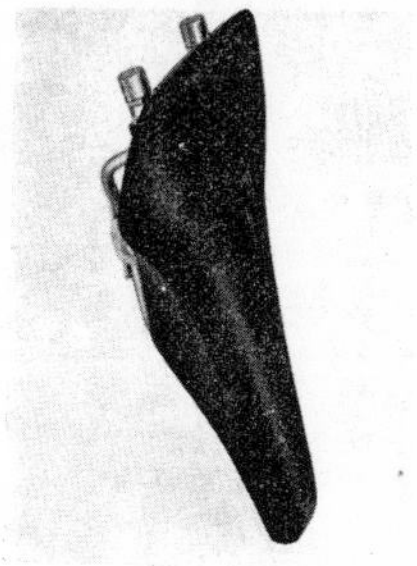

Figure 31

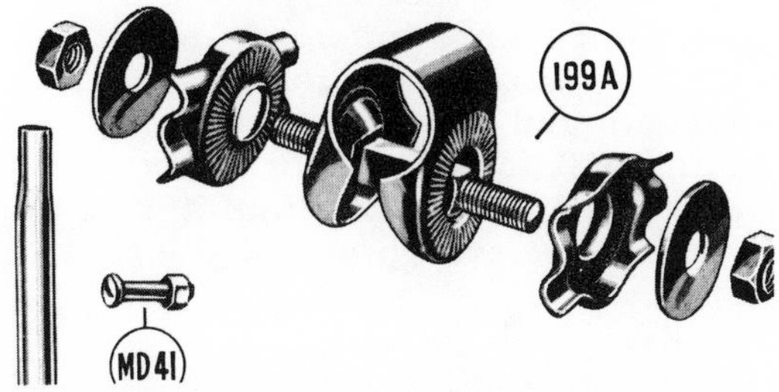

MODEL 750A
GENT'S FULL ROADSTER.

MODEL 750B
GENT'S FULL ROADSTER.

The Fork.

There are two basic style forks. The most popular, mostly because it is less expensive, is the one piece unit with fork legs and stem welded together. The second is either the knee action or spring action, in which the legs are attached to stem section by springs or some means of suspension.

The stem is similiar on both styles and contains the same basic pieces. The handlebar stem fits into the fork system, allowing handlebar steering movement to be transferred down the fork stem, to the fork, and finally, to the front wheel.

Lower fork head cup (S635, figure 32) is stationary and not adjustable. All adjustment to the stem assembly must be made on upper fork head cup.

1. Be sure this assembly is always tight. Wear at this point may be harmful to entire front wheel assembly, especially the bearings.

Figure 32

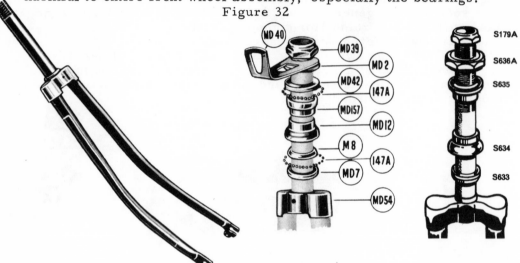

Figure 32 illustrates components in two different fork assemblies.
1. To repair a bent fork, turn your bike upside down.
2. Remove axle locknuts and the front wheel.
3. Apply pressure and pull fork in proper direction to straighten. If a long section of pipe is available, and diameter is correct, slip it over the fork and use leverage to straighten. Make this adjustment in stages to avoid over-adjustment.
4. Installation of fork assembly.
    a. Slip bottom crown race(MD 7, figure 32) on fork stem.
    b. Insert ball bearings(147a) and slip bottom ball race(MD 8) over bearings after liberally greasing the bearing assembly.
    c. Place bottom race cup (MD 12) over other components and slip the stem into place on the frame.
    d. Place top head cup and seating(one piece)(MD 157) in place and install upper bearing unit, after greasing it thoroughly.
    e. Screw top adjusting nut(MD 42) down into place.
    f. Place head locking nut on last, and tighten securely.
    g. Check the fork before replacing front wheel. If it's loose or has any play, or is too tight and doesn't turn freely, re-adjust the upper adjusting nut until correct.

Handlebar and handlebar stem.

The steering assembly consists of the handlebars, handlebar stem(also known as the gooseneck), and the front fork.

There are several different types and each has a distinct purpose. Style and comfort, and function are all important in selecting handlebars.

The rider should fit himself for comfort and be sure handlebars fit his taste before making the purchase.

When placing the handlebars in opening of stem, be certain the knurled section is centralized in stem before tightening the screw.

1. For safety, the handlebars must be tight at all times. If handlebar is moved up and down too often, especially without loosening the screw, the knurled section will wear and won't hold an adjustment.

    a. If knurled area is worn too badly, replace the handlebars.

2. Don't overtighten the collar bolt. You might strip it and break the adjusting collar down in the stem.

3. Don't drop your bike on the handlebars. Dropping will only cause broken or bent handlebars.

4. Always adjust handlebar height at the stem. Secondary adjustment at collar is for tilt or angle. Be sure at least 2 1/2" of stem remains in the frame.

Figure 34

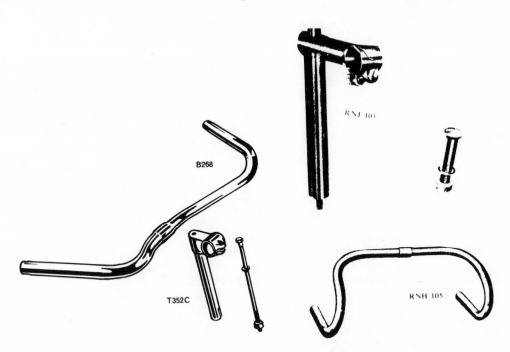

Figure 35
A selection of handlebars for a variety of functions.

	DROP	BEND	WIDTH	CENTER
880	11¾"	5⅞"	26"	1"
879	12¼"	1⅜"	31¼"	1"
870	9¼"	1⅜"	24½"	1"
888	9¾"	5"	20¼"	1"
872	3"	none	24"	1"
877	5¾"	3¹⁵⁄₁₆"	15"	1"
895	3"	2¼"	21"	1"
851	3"	2¼"	21"	¹⁵⁄₁₆"

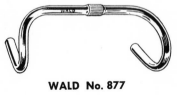

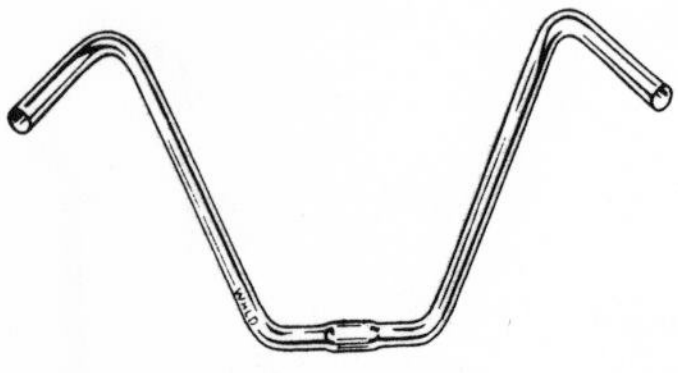

WALD No. 880

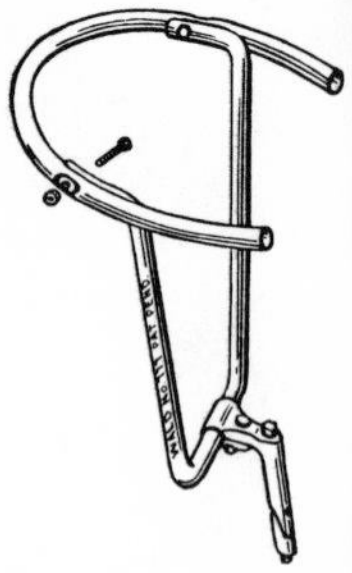

WALD No. 777

WALD No. 879
WALD No. 870

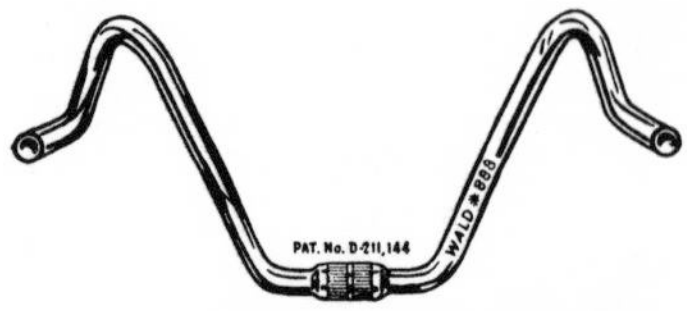

WALD No. 888

WALD No. 872

WALD No. 877

WALD No. 895

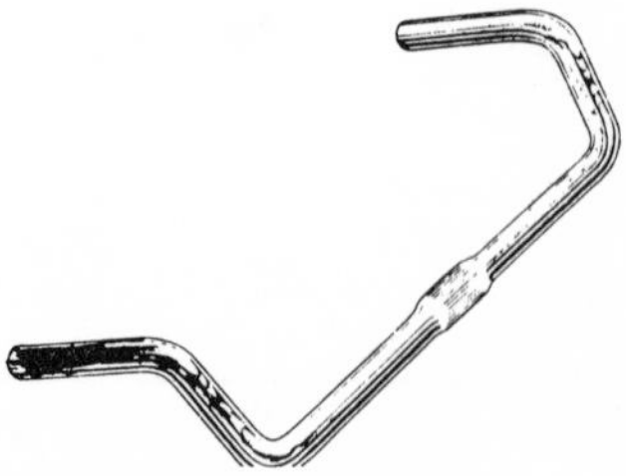

The Handlebar stem.

The stem holds the handlebars in place and fits inside the fork stem, where it functions as an intregal part of the steering process. There are two types of stems. One, figure 36, has a beveled lower portion, which presses against the fork stem when the expander bolt is tightened. The second, as in figure 36a, has expander slots on the lower stem. As the expander bolt is tightened, a plug is drawn up into the stem, forcing it open against the sides of the fork stem.

Figure 36   Figure 36a

If the stem breaks, proceed as follows.
1. Remove the post bolt, which releases upper portion of the stem and handlebars.
2. Replace screw in the plug and turn down a couple of times.
3. Hit the bolt sharply with a hammer or other object. This should free all broken parts from inside the fork stem.
4. Remove all broken parts and replace with new stem. Be sure new part matches broken part. Many stems aren't interchangeable.
5. To replace the part, pull plug, or beveled portion of stem, up as far as it will go without tightening the bolt.
6. Work the stem down into the fork, as you turn handlebars from side to side.
7. After stem is down as far as it will go, tighten the post bolt by turning it counterclockwise. Pushing stem down to extreme will lessen the chance of breaking it.
    a. Use either a 1/2" or 9/16" wrench for majority of bikes. If the size is wrong for your bike, use the adjustable crescent wrench and adjust to size.

Figure 37
Expander bolt with tapered plug.

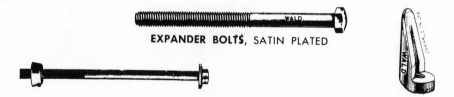

EXPANDER BOLTS, SATIN PLATED

Chapter Five

The Chain and related components.

Bicycle chain is composed of roller links and connecting links. Chain thus formed is called roller chain. Roller chain is used extensively in industry to drive machines, heavy equipment, as lifting agent in hoists and conveying systems, but its biggest usage is on the plain old bike.

There are several different size chains. They are made to match the teeth on the drive sprocket and crank sprocket. Figure 38 illustrates three different type chains currently in use.

Figure 38

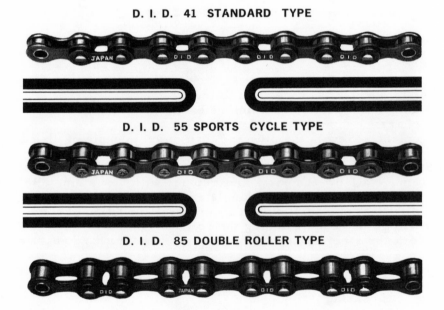

D. I. D. 41 STANDARD TYPE

D. I. D. 55 SPORTS CYCLE TYPE

D. I. D. 85 DOUBLE ROLLER TYPE

The chain is entirely riveted except for the connecting link, where the dis-connecting takes place. Figure 39, on the next page, illustrates three different style connecting links.

If you have chain trouble, and need replacement links, take your old chain to the parts dealer to insure getting an equal. Many chains are not interchangeable.

Figure 39

Snap-on type.   Spring clip type.   Offset type.

Chain problems and sprocket trouble are often mistakenly interchanged. For example, a clicking or grinding sound when cycling under strain, will probably be caused by a worn sprocket, and not a bad chain.

If your chain breaks continually, it's probably due to a worn or bent sprocket.

On the other hand, if the chain jumps off the sprocket frequently, the chain is probably damaged. Locate the damaged roller links and replace them. A bent sprocket will occasionally cause the chain to jump, but the chain will never jump the sprocket because it's too loose.

To service the chain, other than oiling or minor adjustment like tightening, turn your bike upside down.

1. Turn the pedals, and start chain away from sprocket. Unless the chain is too tight, it shouldn't be necessary to move the wheel closer.
2. Turn the pedals to the rear and remove the chain.
3. Pry connecting link apart and remove the chain.
    a. To repair or replace a link, place link over open vise.
    b. Place punch on link and tap it out of post with a hammer.
    c. If necessary, remove all bad links at the same time.
    d. To rejoin the chain, place a link post through link plate and snap into place with a pair of pliers. Plate must go on the outside.
4. To install the chainkeep the bike upside down.
5. Loosen rear wheel if necessary.
    a. Loosen chain adjusters if the bike is so equipped.
6. Move the rear wheel forward as far as it will go, and slip the chain over wheel sprocket.
7. Start chain on bottom crank sprocket. Turn crank toward the rear.
8. Chain will slip easily into place. Tighten chain adjusters, or move rear wheel back as needed. When adjustment is complete, chain should have about 1/2" play midway between crank sprocket and wheel sprocket.
    a. Always assemble the chain before placing it on the bike.

The Crank and Sprocket

There are two basic type cranks. The one piece crank fits through the sprocket and is held in place by a double bearing, adjusting cone system.

The second type utilizes an axle system with separate hanger crank legs for each pedal.

Figure 40, page 36, illustrates the one piece crank and components.

The single hanger leg is best illustrated on page 37.

Figure 40

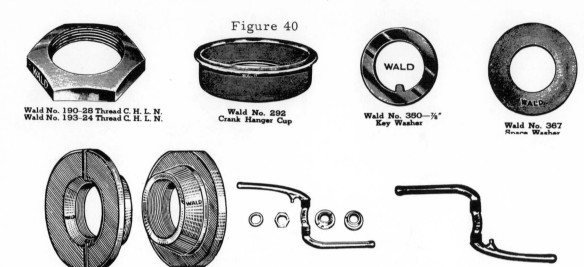

Wald No. 190–28 Thread C. H. L. N.
Wald No. 193–24 Thread C. H. L. N.

Wald No. 292
Crank Hanger Cup

Wald No. 350—⅞″
Key Washer

Wald No. 367
Space Washer

The one piece crank contains one pedal on each end and works in the sprocket where it turns on a pair of bearings through part of the frame and is held in place, and adjusted, by a pair of adjusting cones.

It's vitally important to keep the crank tight at all times. If it works loose, dirt will gather in the bearings and damage the sub-assembly. The key(350), figure 40, prevents the crank from working loose, but when the key wears after crank has worked loose, severe damage will result.

1. To remove crank or sprocket wheel, turn bike upside down.
2. Remove locknut(190) by turning clockwise.
3. Remove key washer(350). Use a screwdriver if necessary.
4. Remove the adjusting cone by turning it off clockwise.
5. Remove bearing assemblies, both sides, before removing crank.
6. If the crank is bent, place end in a vise and straighten as needed.
7. If crank eyes are stripped, and pedals keep working out, check your local machine shop for a tapping tool. Your dan might have one in his tool kit. Check for proper size thread and re-tap the crank as needed. However, if you re-tap, you might have to replace the pedals. If threads are badly worn, replace the entire crank.
8. If a pedal breaks in the crank, try drilling the broken part out, and follow above steps for re-tapping. If you can't do a neat job, replace the crank.

Reverse the above steps to replace the crank assembly.

1. Grease both bearing units before replacing.
2. Check all components. Replace all damaged or broken parts.
3. Put the first bearing, flat side first, agains the sprocket cone.
4. Replace the crank in frame.
5. Replace second bearing over crank, with beveled side in, and place it against the retaining cup.
6. Replace second cone and turn to left until tight, then back it off.
7. Replace the key washer.
8. Replace the locknut and tighten securely.
9. Use caution when replacing the components. If the crank turns when lock nut is tightened, replace the key washer.

Follow the above steps for installing components on one piece hanger unit, except removal. The hanger is held in place with a roll pin. Knock it out with a punch and hammer. See figure 41, page 37.

Figure 41

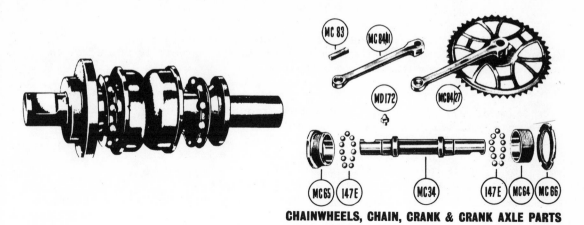

CHAINWHEELS, CHAIN, CRANK & CRANK AXLE PARTS

The crank sprocket is driven by pedal action, which activates the chain and travels back to the rear wheel sprocket, which drives the bicycle.

Sprockets vary in size and number of teeth, according to the type of chain used. Bikes used solely for pleasure utilize a different sprocket drive than the racer. Multi-gear units use a different sprocket than a child's sidewalk bike.

The main thing to remember when ordering a replacement is, the chain size and number of sprocket teeth must match.

If removal is necessary, refer to page 36.

Removal is necessary if;

1. The sprocket is bent or broken.
2. Chain keeps falling off.
3. If the bike is hard to pump, and other assemblies are functioning.
   a. If the sprocket is bent, straighten in a bench vise.
   b. If not bent too badly, try correcting it on the bike, using a pair of pliers, or a pipe wrench.

Figure 42

A selection of sprocket chainwheels   Single hanger type crank-wheel.

Wald No 712
52 t. x ¼" x ½"

Wald No. 718
48 t. x ⅛" x ½"

Wald No. 536
36 t. x ⅛" x ½"

Pedals.

Figure 43 illustrates the basic components of the pedal.

Pedal action is quite important and since they're generally subjected to the most abuse, a few tips should be helpful.

1. The pedals turn on a series of cones and bearings (MH 14, 147B) on the center axle(MH 67). The pedal is connected to the crank by threaded axle(MH 67). Since the axle carries most of the weight, breakage at the crank is common. See crank adjustment, page 36.

2. Pedals are marked for proper installation.
    a. Pedals marked "L" are installed in the left crank.
    b. Pedals marked "R" are installed in right crank.

3. When pedals become broken or bent, replace them.

4. Keep your pedals tight at all times. Loose pedals are dangerous.

Figure 43

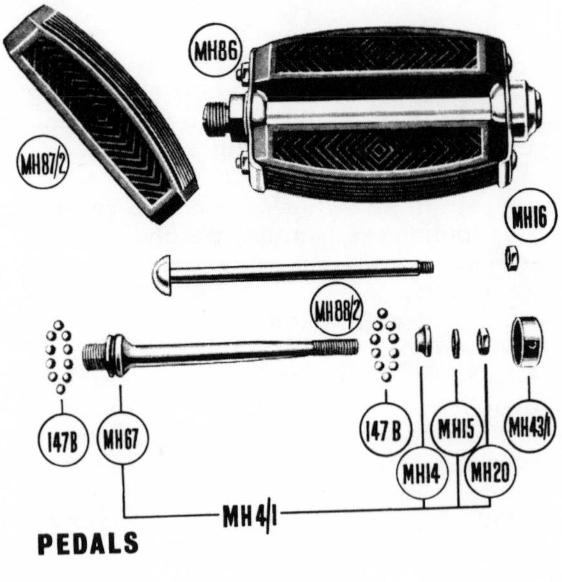

PEDALS

Chapter Six

The Coaster Brake and Caliper Brake.

The coaster brake is possibly the most intricate part of the bicycle. Proper care of this sub-assembly may add years to the life of the average bike. A little oil occasionally, plus a quick inspection of all nuts, and a check of the wheel alignment, will save many costly repair bills.

At one time New Departure division of General Motors, Morrow and the Bendix Corporation, supplied most of the coaster brakes sold on American made bikes. That's all changed. Many bicycles are imported and coaster brakes are manufactured by various companies around the world. We have tried to cover the more popular and most widely used models.

Bikes equipped with coaster brakes are easy to identify. They have the arm and brake clip attachment.

Figure 44
The coaster brake illustrated in ghost form.

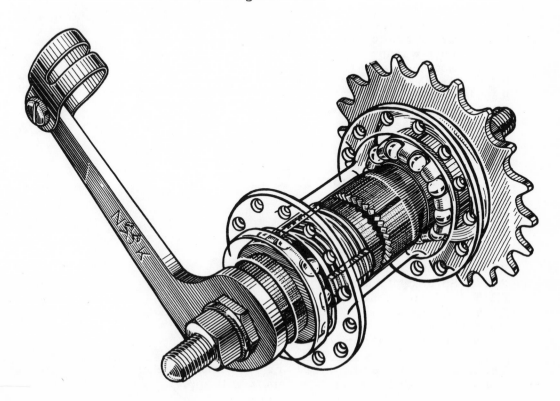

Figure 45 illustrates the components of a Resilion Coaster brake hub assembly. The Resilion is made in France and comes as standard equipment on a variety of bicycles.

Figure 45

Resilion Coaster Hub.

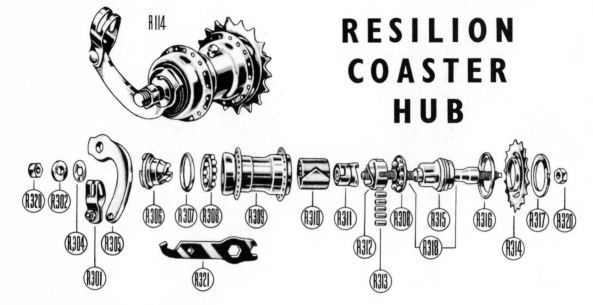

R301   Brake arm clip
R301A   Brake arm clip nut and bolt
R302   Lock washer
R304   Notched washer
R305   Brake arm
R306   Brake cone
R307   Left hand dust cover
R308   Ball cage & balls
R309   Hub shell
R309A   shell lubricator
R310   Brake cylinder
R311   Hub brake actuator
R312   Roller guide ring
R313   Rollers, drive
R314   Sprocket
R315   Driving sleeve
R315A   Driving sleeve split ring
R316   Right hand dust cover
R317   Sprocket lock ring
R318   Axle and cone
R319   Washer
R320   Axle lock nuts
R321   Service spanner wrench

The Resilion coaster hub functions very much like most coaster brakes and service tips from next several units will apply.

If your bike is hard to pump when riding on level ground, or doesn't coast smoothly, the problem is probably in the coaster brake. This assembly is not as complicated as it looks and the average boy should be able to service it easily.

1. Check the tire and wheel assembly. If the wheel is out of line, refer to the chapter covering the wheel and service as needed.

2. If the brake squeals or makes a rubbing noise, a few drops of oil will solve the problem. Use a good grade oil.

3. If the bike hasn't been greased frequently, or if you're buying a used bike and aren't sure of its condition, lubricate bearings(R307 & 308, fig. 45).

4. Recheck rear axle nuts(R320). If they're loose, tighten them.

5. If the brake locks(will not allow wheel to move in either direction), loosen axle nuts(R320) and re-adjust adjusting cone outward. If the adjusting cone is badly worn, replace it.

6. To dis-assemble the unit, remove axle nuts, chain from sprocket, and pull the rear wheel away from bike.

Figure 46

Morrow Coaster Brake-parts breakdown.

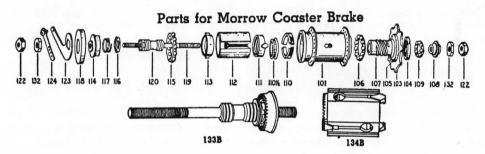

Parts for Morrow Coaster Brake

122 132 124 123 118 114 117 116   120 115 119   113   112   111 110½ 110   101   106 107 105 103 104 109 108 132 122

133B   134B

There are still some Morrow coaster brakes around and the following service tips might help.

A Morrow coaster brake is activated and propels the bike when the rider moves the pedal, which activates the chain and drives the sprocket. When the sprocket turns, the clutch rings expand forcing them against the end of the hub.

If the bike starts slipping, instead of pulling steady, check the coaster brake assembly.

1. Check clutch rings (110). If they are wrong, or if sleeve expander (111), is damaged and can't force rings against the hub, the unit will slip.

2. Check driver-sprocket assembly. If damaged, replace components. If the bike pumps hard, check the brake sleeve(112), it could be dragging against the hub. If damaged, replace it.

When dis-assembling the coaster brake always start at the sprocket end.

1. Remove the adjusting cone completely away from axle.

2. Tighten lock nut on brake side to prevent brake from turning during dismantling.

3. Remove components as required.

4. Always protect threads with cloth if pliers are used to hold axle.

Re-assembly, Morrow Coaster Brake.

1. Check adjusting cone on the brake side and note two slots. The axle bushing has two fingers and they must slide into the slots, which holds the cone in a stationary position.
2. Screw axle bushing(120) onto axle(119) until fingers are flush on end of axle.
3. Slip washer(116) in place, small end goes on first.
4. Hold cone(114) and place spring(117) with ends of spring away from cone slots, and holding washer with your fingers, press down on spring and slip bushing into cone slots and place it on the axle.
5. Screw inward until it extends about one inch beyond cone.
6. Slip dust cover(118) in place, add the brake arm(123) and tighten the lock nut(132). Figure 46, sub assembly 133b illustrates complete unit.
After you finish with the sub-assembly, turn to the brake sleeve parts. The assembly(134B) contains components(111, 112, and 113).

1. To assemble, place retaining ring(110 1/2) under fingers of expander (111).
2. Place clutch rings(110) on retaining ring, hold clutch rings in place and place onto the hub.
3. Grease bearings(115) and slip in place with balls facing inward.
4. Insert cone/axle assembly, and turn wheel over.
5. Grease bearings(106) and install with balls facing inward.
6. Screw(103-105-107) driving assembly into place.
7. Place other adjusting cone(108) into place on unit.
8. Finish assembly by screwing locknut(132) into place.
    a. Hold adjusting cone and tighten locknut securely. If the locknut works loose, severe damage may result to the assembly.
Check your job. If wheel turns in sluggish manner, loosen the adjusting cone slightly. If wheel is too loose, tighten adjusting cone as needed.

New Departure.

New Departure brake model D is illustrated below in component form. Many replacement parts for older brakes may be obtained from foreign makers of bicycle parts.

Figure 47

Parts for Model "D" New Departure Coaster Brake

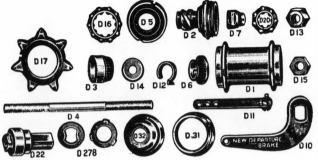

No.	Description
D 2	Driver, threaded type . . . .
D 3	Clutch Sleeve . . . .
D 4	Axle (6½" x ⅜") . . . .
D 5	Sprocket Set Nut, threaded type . . . .
D 6	Brake Clutch . . . .
D 7	Axle Adjusting Cone . . . .
D 10	Brake Arm . . . .
D 11	Clip Nut and Bolt, complete . . . . . .
D 12	Transfer Spring . . . .
D 13	Axle Nut . . . .
D 14	Axle Washer . . . .
D 15	Lock Nut . . . .
D 16	Large Ball Retainer (Ten ¼" balls) . .
D 17	Sprocket, threaded type, 10 tooth
	18, 19 and 20 tooth
D 20	Small Ball Retainer (Seven ¼" balls) .
D 22	Disc Support Sleeve . . . .
D278	Brake Disc Set (17 bronze and steel) .
D 31	Dust Cap, sprocket end . . . .
D 32	Dust Cap, brake arm end . . . .

Assembly-New Departure brake.

1. Place disc support sleeve(D22) on axle(D4).
2. Place disc support assembly dust cap(D32), brake arm(D10),and the lock nut(D 15) on axle.
3. Place spring(D 12) on brake clutch(D6). Long tip of spring must point away from brake clutch teeth.
4. Slide brake clutch (d6) into clutch sleeve (D3) and place spring into proper groove.
5. After clutch sleeve assembly is in place, install the brake disc set complete. Alternate components. One without teeth first, then another with teeth, and so on until complete. Last disc shouldn't have teeth if assembly is correct. Install on unit(D22).
6. Slide bearing unit in place with balls pointing inward. To insure long life, grease bearings frequently.
7. Insert disc support assembly(D22).
8. Slide the second bearing into place.
9. Sprocket-drive assembly should be screwed into place.
10. Adjusting cone should be installed next. Screw inward until there's no play in the wheel.
11. Install axle nut. Hold adjusting cone with one wrench while screwing axle nut on tightly. Use a locknut on the axle. Plain nut will work loose and damage the coaster brake assembly.

Figure 48

Figure 49

The Mattatuck Coaster Brake.
The Model E is a New Departure style assembly.

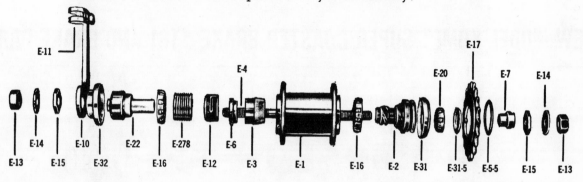

Centrix Coaster Brake.

Figure 50 illustrates the Centrix brake by components, and as a unit. You'll notice all coaster brakes contain about the same number, and type, parts. Service procedures on one style will generally apply to another, except in the case of multi-speed units.

Figure 50

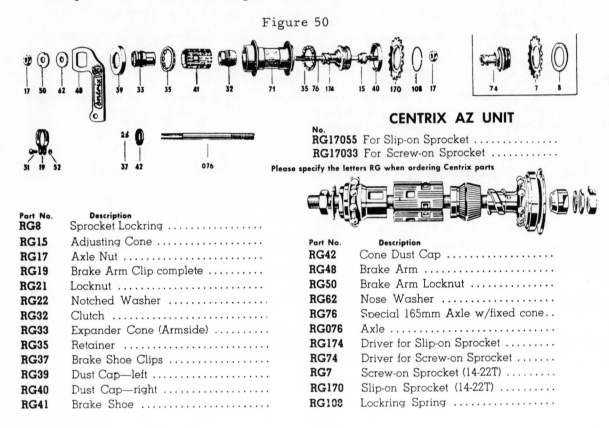

CENTRIX AZ UNIT

No.
RG17055 For Slip-on Sprocket ....
RG17033 For Screw-on Sprocket ....
Please specify the letters RG when ordering Centrix parts

Part No.	Description		Part No.	Description	
RG8	Sprocket Lockring		RG42	Cone Dust Cap	
RG15	Adjusting Cone		RG48	Brake Arm	
RG17	Axle Nut		RG50	Brake Arm Locknut	
RG19	Brake Arm Clip complete		RG62	Nose Washer	
RG21	Locknut		RG76	Special 165mm Axle w/fixed cone..	
RG22	Notched Washer		RG076	Axle	
RG32	Clutch		RG174	Driver for Slip-on Sprocket	
RG33	Expander Cone (Armside)		RG74	Driver for Screw-on Sprocket	
RG35	Retainer		RG7	Screw-on Sprocket (14-22T)	
RG37	Brake Shoe Clips		RG170	Slip-on Sprocket (14-22T)	
RG39	Dust Cap—left		RG108	Lockring Spring	
RG40	Dust Cap—right				
RG41	Brake Shoe				

Figure 50a

The Komet brake illustrated below features the brake cylinder brake. Fewer working parts make the unit less troublesome.

NEW MODEL KOMET SUPER COASTER BRAKE #161 AND BRAKE PART

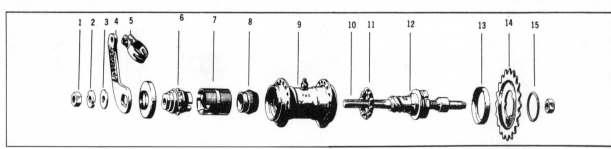

The Perry model B-100 coaster brake.

The Perry B-100 unit can be interchanged with Sturmey-Archer units.
Figure 51

The Perry B-100 Coaster Brake

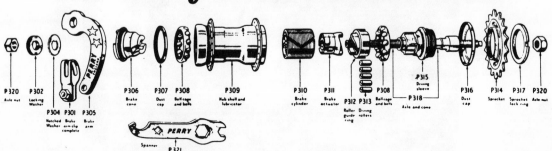

Figure 52
The Perry B-500 Juvenile Coaster Brake.

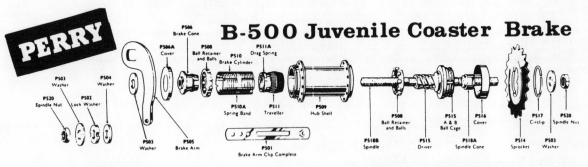

No.	Description		No.	Description
P 505	Brake Arm		P 510A	Spring Band
P 506	Adjustable Brake Cone		P 511	Traveller (Actuator)
P 506A	Dust Cover		P 515	Driver
P 508	Ball Retainer and Balls		P 516	Dust Cover
P 510	Brake Cylinder		P 518	Axle and Stationary Cone Complete

The Bendix.

The Bendix 70.

Figure 53

To assemble the Bendix unit the following general instructions will apply to most of their line.
1. Before assembly, always grease bearings(BB 16).
2. Screw expander(BB59) onto axle.
3. Slip dust cap on arm side(BB32), brake arm(10), and lock nut in place and tighten lock nut firmly. Place sub-assembly aside temporarily.
4. Place retarder spring(BB112) and expander(BB56) with slots facing inward on axle.
5. Insert brake shoe keys(BB51) between arm side expander and expander retarder.
6. Install brake shoes between the keys.
7. Place clutch(BB53) into place.
8. Place sub-assembly into hub. Hold brake shoes so they don't slip.
9. Slip bearing(BB16) into place, with balls pointing inward.
10. Place driving assembly(BB52, BB58, BB60-64), in position.
11. Install second bearing with balls pointing inward toward sprocket.
12. Screw adjusting cone into place and check for proper adjustment, before screwing lock nut on axle. If wheel turns in sluggish manner, loosen adjusting cone slightly. If excess play is present, tighten cone as needed.
13. Screw lock nut in place and tighten firmly. Hold cone with wrench and tighten lock nut with another.

Figure 54
Bendix Brake assembly-Model RB

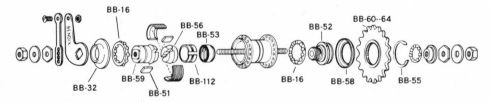

Figure 55
Bendix Model 70-parts breakdown.

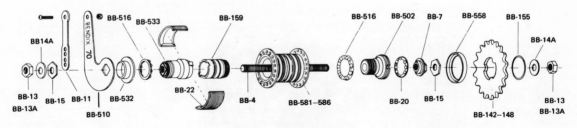

Bendix Model 70-J. Parts breakdown.

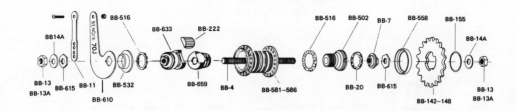

Figure 56
Original Bendix.

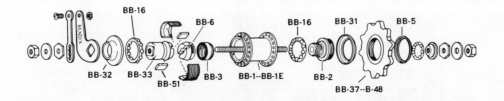

Figure 57
Early model Bendix 2-speed automatic. From 1960 to 1964

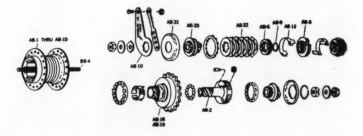

Figure 57a
Later model Bendix two-speed automatic with shoe brakes. Made after 1-1965 to present. The new unit is color coded yellow.

This New 2-SPEED AUTOMATIC with
Shoe Brake is identified by 3 yellow
color bands on hub shell

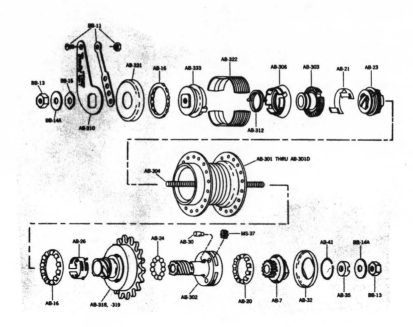

Sturmey Archer Coaster Brake.

Figure 58

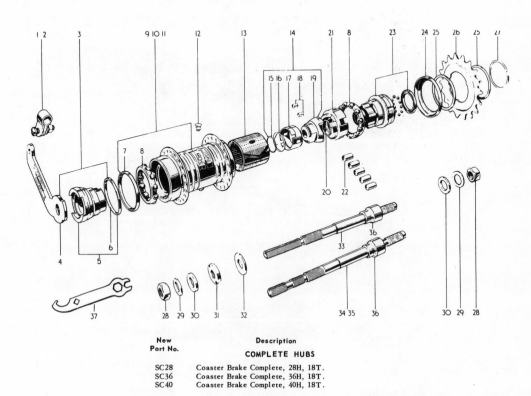

New Part No.	Description
	COMPLETE HUBS
SC28	Coaster Brake Complete, 28H, 18T.
SC36	Coaster Brake Complete, 36H, 18T.
SC40	Coaster Brake Complete, 40H, 18T.

New Part No.	Description	New Part No.	Description
1 HSL733	Chainstay Clip Complete - Sports...	24 HSL735	Sprocket Dust Cover ....
2 HSL732	Chainstay Clip Complete - Roadster .	25 HMW127	Sprocket Washers (2 off)........
3 HSH426	Torque Arm Assembly	26 HSL716	16T x 1/8" Sprockets ....
4 HSH424	Torque Arm	26 HSL717	17T x 1/8" Sprockets ....
5 HSH438	Brake Cone Assembly	26 HSL718	18T x 1/8" Sprockets ....
6 HSH429	Cone Dust Cover .... Per 10	26 HSL719	19T x 1/8" Sprockets ....
7 HSH439	Shell Dust Cover .... Per 10	26 HSL720	20T x 1/8" ....
8 HSH427	Ball Cage Complete...........	27 HSL721	Circlip ....
9 HSH421	Hub Shell Complete 40H........	28 HMN118	Axle Nut (2 off) ....
10 HSH422	Hub Shell Complete 36H........	29 HMW146	Axle Washer 1/16" (2 off). . Per Doz.
11 HSH423	Hub Shell Complete 28H........	30 HMW129	Axle Washer 1/8" (2 off) ......
12 HSA167	Lubricator	31 HMN257	L. H. Brake Arm Nut ....
13 HSH436	Brake Band Complete..........	32 HMW366	Tongued Washer .... Per 10
14 HSH440	Actuator Assembly	33 HSH419	6¼" Axle Complete with Fixed Cone Standard ....
15 HSH435	Actuator Circlip .... Per 10	34 HSH420	6½" Axle Complete with Fixed Cone. Suitable for Raleigh Ind. Bicycles ..
16 HMW365	Roller Retainer Washer..... Per 10	35 HSH418	6 7/8" Axle Complete with Fixed Cone. Suitable for Raleigh Ind. Bicycles.....
17 HSH434	Actuator Roller Retainer		
18 HSH433	Actuator Rollers (2 off)	36 HSH441	R. H. Fixed Cone ....
19 HSH432	Actuator	37 HSL734	Spanner ....
20 HSH431	Driver Circlip .... Per 10		
21 HSH430	Roller Retainer, Driver		
22 HSH428	Driver Rollers (5 off)...... Per 10		
23 HSH425	Driver Complete with Balls.......		

Sturmey Archer 3 speed axle and coaster brake unit.

Figure 59

MARK 3

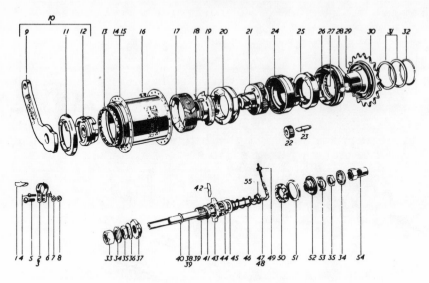

New Part No.	Old Part No.	Description
1 HSH-401	P-1735	Strengthening Pad (Sports Machines Only) . . . .
2 HSL-709	K-321	Clip for Brake Arm (Roadster)
3 HSL-710	K-320	Clip for Brake Arm (Sports) .
4 HMB-102	X-69	Clip Screw-3/16'' diam. . . .
5 HMB-137	X-69A	Clip Screw-¼'' diam. . . . . .
6 HMN-105	S-524	Clip Screw Nut (for 3/16'' Screw) . . . . Per 10
7 HMW-157	GL-432	Shakeproof Washer . . . . . .
8 HMN-139	K-175	Clip Screw Nut (for ¼'' Screw) . . . . Per 10
9 HSH-402	K-317	Brake Arm . . . .
10 HSH-403	KQ-5	Brake Arm/L.H. Cone/Dust Cap Assembly . . . .
11 HSH-404	K-316	Dust Cap for L.H. Cone . . .
12 HSH-405	K-315	L.H. Cone . . . .
13 HSA-164	KQ-4	Ball Cage (18) 3/16'' Ball .
14 HSA-165	KQ-3	Shell and Ball Cup Assembly-40 hole. . . . .
15 HSA-166	KQ-3A	Shell and Ball Cup Assembly-36 hole . . . .
16 HSA-167	K-645	Lubricator (Steel) . . . . . .
17 HSH-406	KQ-2	Brake Band . . . .
18 HSH-407	K-308	Brake Actuating Spring . . .
19 HSH-408	K-309	Thrust Plate . . . .
20 HSA-168	KQ-1	Planet Cage Pawl Ring . . .
21 HSA-169	K-302	Planet Cage . . . .
22 HSA-115	K-16	Planet Pinion . . . .
23 HSA-170	K-483A	Pinion Pin . . . . . . Per 10
24 HSA-171	K-322	Gear Ring . . . .
25 HSA-172	K-485Z	Gear Ring Pawl Ring . . . .
26 HSA-121	K-60	R.H. Ball Ring. . . . .
27 HSA-122	K-63	Inner Dust Cap. . . . Per 10
28 HSA-123	K-462	Driver . . . .
29 HSL-701	K-62	Sprocket Dust Cap . . . . . .
30 SEE AW HUB		Sprocket 16-20T and 22T . .
31 HMW-127	X-49	Sprocket Spacing Washer-1/16''
32 HSL-721	K-463	Sprocket Circlip . . . .
33 HMN-128	K-520	L.H. Axle Nut . . . .
34 HMW-155	K-536	Serrated Axle Washer. . . . .
35 HMN-132	K-47A	Cone Locknut . . . .
36 HMW-156	K-319	Lockwasher . . . .
37 HMN-135	K-318	Brake Arm Locknut . . . . . .
38 HSA-173	K-300	Axle-5¾'' . . . .
39 HSA-174	K-301	Axle-6¼'' . . . .
40 HSL-725	K-303	Axle Circlip . . . .
41 HSA-116	K-527	Clutch Sleeve . . . .
42 HSA-124	K-526	Axle Key . . . . Per 10
43 HSA-117	K-505A	Clutch . . . .
44 HSA-127	K-528A	Thrust Ring . . . .
45 HMW-148	K-411	Thrust Washer . . . .
46 HSA-128	K-530A	Clutch Spring. . . . . Per 10
47 HSA-129	K-529	Clutch Spring Cap. . Per 10
48 HSA-125	K-504Z	Indicator Coupling for 5¾'' Axle . . . .
49 HSA-126	K-504AZ	Indicator Coupling for 6¼'' Axle . . . .
50 HMN-134	K-227	Connection Lock Nut Per 10
51 HSA-103	K-67Z	Ball Cage (18¼'' balls) . . .
52 HSA-102	LB-405	Dust Cap . . . .
53 HSA-101	K-506Z	R.H. Cone with Dust Cap . .
54 HMW-147	K-516	R.H. Cone Lock Washer . . . . Per 10
55 HMN-129	K-519	R.H. Axle Nut . . . .

To service the Sturmey Archer TCW Mark 3, dismantle as follows.
1. Remove rear wheel rom bike.
2. Grip sprocket end of axle firmly. Use a shop vise if available.
3. Remove locknut(33), axle washer(34), and brake arm nut(37).
4. Lift away the brake arm(9), and left cone assembly(10).
5. Remove ball bearing unit(13) and pull out the brake band(17).
   a. Left hand ball is pressed into the hub shell and must be removed as a unit.
6. Turn wheel over and remove balance of parts from other side.
7. To insure proper re-assembly. look for letters SA in notches of the right hand bearing ring. Mark the spoke closest to marked notch so the right hand ball ring will be replaced in the same position. The unit has a two-start thread. If not re-assembled properly, the wheel will require re-alignment.
8. Loosen right ball race(26) with a light tap on one of notches, using a punch and hammer.
9. Hold the wheel and withdraw balance of components as a unit.
10. Remove brake thrust plate(19), and planet cage pawl ring(20).
11. Place left end of axle in a vise(use caution and don't damage part), remove right axle locknut(33), washers, cone lock washer(50), and the right cone(33).
12. Remove clutch spring (46), driver and sprocket(28-30), right hand ball ring(26), gear ring pawl(25), and gear ring(24).
13. Remove thrust washer(45), and thrust ring(44).
14. Unscrew indicator rod(48).
15. Remove axle key(42) and remove sliding clutch and sleeve(41-42).
16. Remove pinion pins(42), and remove the pinion.
After unit is dismantled, check individual sections for possible trouble.
1. Sliding clutch should slide up and down easily.
2. Check alignment of axle.
3. Check sprocket gear for broken or chipped teeth.
4. Check all raceways for wear or scratched surface.
5. Check pinion pins on sliding clutch and gear ring splines for wear at engaging points.
6. Check pawl and pawl ratchet for wear.
   a. To replace pawls and springs in planet cage pawl ring, fit the spring, pawl and pin per diagram below. Support pawl pin head on piece of steel held in a vise. Pawl pin must be riveted over, without distorting the head.

Figure 60   Figure 61

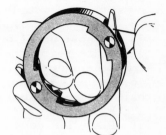

b. To replace pawls and springs in gear ring pawl ring, fit a pawl spring into pawl ring per figure 60, on preceding page. File the pin end so it doesn't stick out beyond edge of ring. Turn the pawl back as far as possible and insert tail of spring between pawl ring and pawl pin. Fit bent end of the spring under shorter end of pawl. Return pawl to proper position.

Before you can re-assemble balance of this hub it's necessary to form three additional sub-assemblies.

1. Fit ball cage into driver, with ring of ball retainer facing outward. If you replace the ball retainer, replace the dust cap also.

2. Fit inner dust cap to right ball ring. Be sure balls move freely when dust caps are mounted in place.

3. Press dust cap over left adjusting cone. Slots in dust cap must fit over slots in cone. Press brake arm tightly into left cone slots. Sturmey Archer etching must face outward.

4. After pawls have been assembled, grease all moveable components. Proceed with additional sub-assembly work.

1. Hold right end of axle in a vise and position until axle key is below the pinion, and fit it into the planet cage, worm up, before pushing retaining ring into axle groove.

2. Turn unit around and place other end of axle in the vise. Add planet pinion(22), and pins(23), with flat end of pins facing downward.

3. Place sleeve, flange first, sliding clutch with slot over the flange of sleeve and axle key (flat of key facing up), and screw the indicator rod into place until all components are in proper position.

4. Insert thrust ring and washer, fitting flat ends of key into slots of the thrust ring.

5. Fit gear ring and gear pawl ring unit(already assembled), into place with pawl pin heads facing up.

6. Replace right ball ring unit.

7. Replace driver sub-assembly.

8. Place clutch spring over axle.

9. Screw right adjusting cone up finger tight, then back it off a half turn before locking it in position with lock washer and locknut.

   a. Use caution when making this adjustment. If the cone is backed away more than one half turn, it could throw entire gear mechanism out of adjustment.

10. Remove unit from vise and place other end in vise. Spray some oil into the planet cage.

11. Fit planet cage pawl ring assembly into place over flat on pinion pins.

12. The brake thrust plate goes next, and leg of brake activating spring must face up, with thrust plate slots engaging planet cage pawl ring dogs.

13. Place brake band on unit, with inner band projections facing up.

14. Remove unit from the vise.

15. Place rear wheel in your lap and insert completed unit into place , from the underside. Screw the right ball ring up finger tight.

16. Recheck marked spoke with marked SA notch. When aligned, screw ball ring up firmly.

17. Place ball race, with balls facing down, into the left ball cup.

18. Place left cone and brake arm assembly on the unit.

   a. Brake band projection and activating spring leg must fit into the respective slots on the cone. Best way to make sure is to turn the spring leg to a right angle with the brake band projection.

19. Place brake arm nut, lock washer, and lock nut into position. Adjust hub bearing until there is just a slight amount of play.

20. If the sprocket was removed from the driver during dismantling, fit outer dust cap over driver before replacing sprocket. Dust cap must be centered properly on the driver flange. Replace sprocket, and spacing washers, in proper order, following dismantling instructions.

21. Replace wheel in bike frame and tighten axle nuts firmly. The brake arm clip will be in position on left chain guide of the bike.

22. If the gear requires adjustment, place control lever in center gear.
    a. To adjust, loosen locknut(C) figure 62, above the chain and rotate knurled connection rod(B) until end of indicator rod is flush with end of axle(see inset(A). When rod is properly set, tighten locknut.

Figure 62

Caliper Brakes.

Caliper front or rear wheel brakes are hand activated and generally on bikes with multi-speed gears. The caliper brake is controlled with a hand lever, which when activated, squeezes two arms inward against the wheel, forcing the wheel to slow, and finally stop by friction.

Most caliper brakes can be adjusted in the same manner. The unit below is manufactured by Hercules Cycle & Motor Company Ltd.

1. Proper adjustment finds brake blocks slightly away from wheel rim and equal distant on each side.

2. To adjust, loosen locknut(Y) on adjuster(Z). Turn adjuster(Z) until the brake blocks are slightly away from rim. Tighten locknut(Y).

3. If the unit required more adjusting, unscrew locknut(Y), screw the adjuster completely in, and loosen the nut holding cable end. Pull cable through the bolt with one hand, and hold brake against rim with the other. Tighten the nut holding the cable and proceed with steps 2, above.

4. If the brake arms are too loose, or too tight, adjust by loosening nut (X) figure 63a & figure 63. Nut(X) holds brake unit to the frame. With a screwdriver in one hand, adjust brake by turning the bolt as needed, and tighten nut(X) with other hand, while holding bolt firmly in place.

Figure 63   Figure 63a

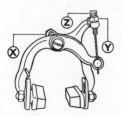 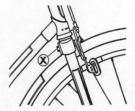

Figure 64
Weinmann style caliper hand brake-component parts and nomenclature.

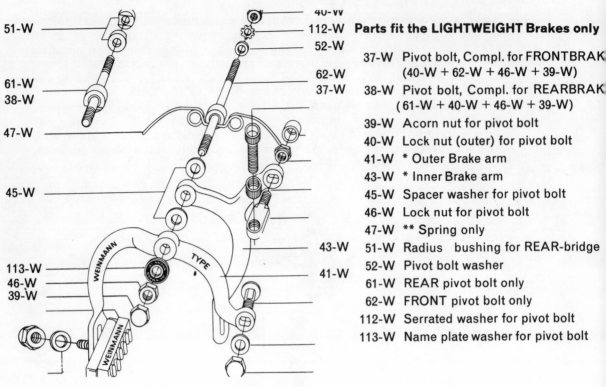

Parts fit the LIGHTWEIGHT Brakes only

37-W Pivot bolt, Compl. for FRONTBRAK
     (40-W + 62-W + 46-W + 39-W)

38-W Pivot bolt, Compl. for REARBRAK
     (61-W + 40-W + 46-W + 39-W)

39-W Acorn nut for pivot bolt

40-W Lock nut (outer) for pivot bolt

41-W * Outer Brake arm

43-W * Inner Brake arm

45-W Spacer washer for pivot bolt

46-W Lock nut for pivot bolt

47-W ** Spring only

51-W Radius bushing for REAR-bridge

52-W Pivot bolt washer

61-W REAR pivot bolt only

62-W FRONT pivot bolt only

112-W Serrated washer for pivot bolt

113-W Name plate washer for pivot bolt

Figure 65
Handlever components for a typical caliper brake assembly-Weinmann.

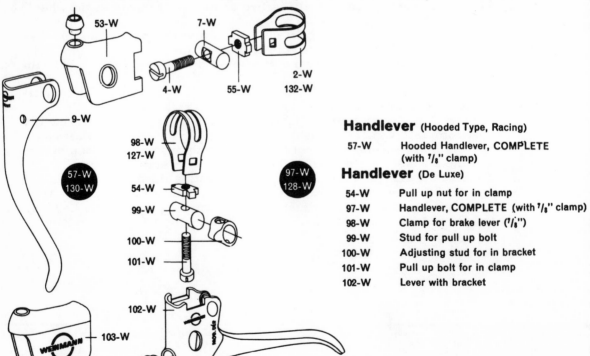

Handlever (Hooded Type, Racing)

57-W Hooded Handlever, COMPLETE
     (with 7/8'' clamp)

Handlever (De Luxe)

54-W Pull up nut for in clamp

97-W Handlever, COMPLETE (with 7/8'' clamp)

98-W Clamp for brake lever (7/8'')

99-W Stud for pull up bolt

100-W Adjusting stud for in bracket

101-W Pull up bolt for in clamp

102-W Lever with bracket

Figure 66
Standard Weinmann caliper brake-- The Phillips caliper brake assembly

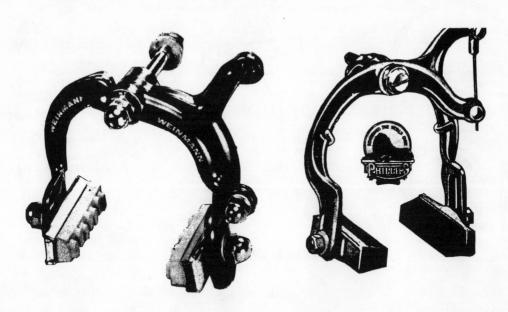

Figure 67
The Weinmann symmetric-action center pull brake for racer bikes.

No. 1022R

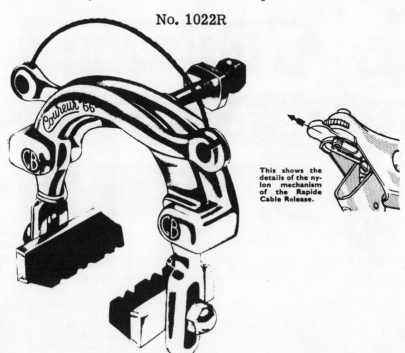

This shows the details of the ny-lon mechanism of the Rapide Cable Release.

Figure 68
The AMF Hercules style caliper brake assembly, models 400 and 401.

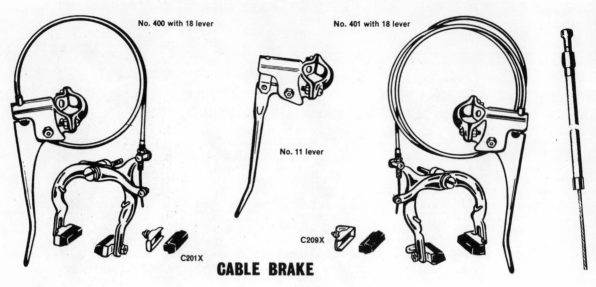

No. 400 with 18 lever

No. 401 with 18 lever

No. 11 lever

C201X

C209X

CABLE BRAKE

Figure 69
Excel caliper brake assembly- Two models will fit most American models

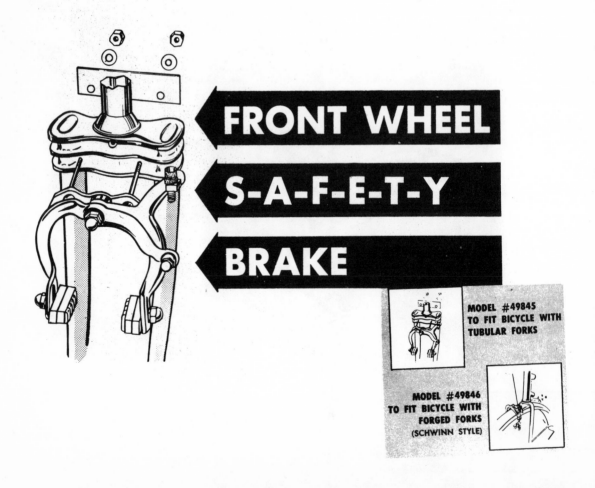

FRONT WHEEL

S-A-F-E-T-Y

BRAKE

MODEL #49845
TO FIT BICYCLE WITH
TUBULAR FORKS

MODEL #49846
TO FIT BICYCLE WITH
FORGED FORKS
(SCHWINN STYLE)

Simple adjustment procedure for the caliper brake.
1.   Loosen knurled ring(A), figure 69a.
2.   Turn adjuster screw(B) counterclockwise until blocks clear rim.
3.   Tighten knurled ring(A).
4.   If one block is closer to the rim, tap opposite coil of spring at (C).
5.   Nut(E) must be tight and blocks must not touch tire when brakes are applied.   Block must touch rim only.
6.   Closed end of brake block must face front of cycle.
7.   If your bike brake has cable anchor pins, nuts and washers, further adjustment can be made by loosening nut(F), figure 69b.
   a.   Move wire in proper direction to correct.   Tighten nut(F).

Figure 69a   Figure 69b

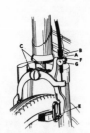

Chapter Seven

The Three, and Five speed axle assembly.

Figure 70

STURMEY ARCHER A.

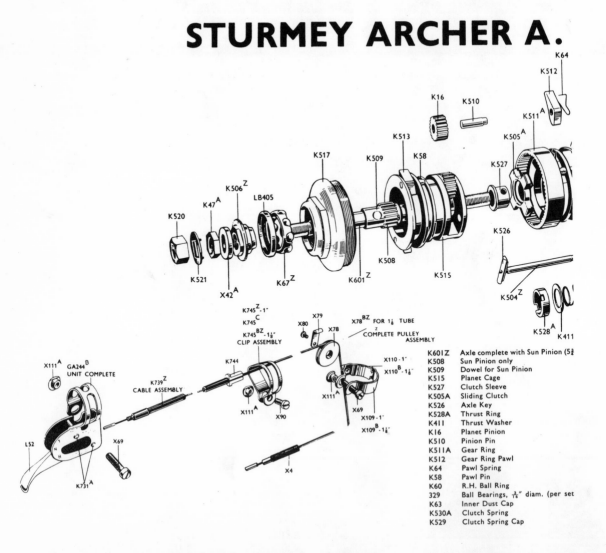

K601Z	Axle complete with Sun Pinion (5¾
K508	Sun Pinion only
K509	Dowel for Sun Pinion
K515	Planet Cage
K527	Clutch Sleeve
K505A	Sliding Clutch
K526	Axle Key
K528A	Thrust Ring
K411	Thrust Washer
K16	Planet Pinion
K510	Pinion Pin
K511A	Gear Ring
K512	Gear Ring Pawl
K64	Pawl Spring
K58	Pawl Pin
K60	R.H. Ball Ring
329	Ball Bearings, $\frac{7}{16}$" diam. (per set
K63	Inner Dust Cap
K530A	Clutch Spring
K529	Clutch Spring Cap

Figure 71

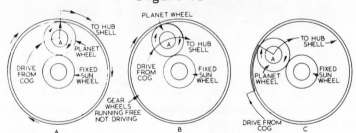

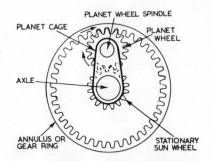

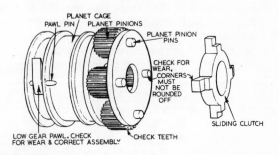

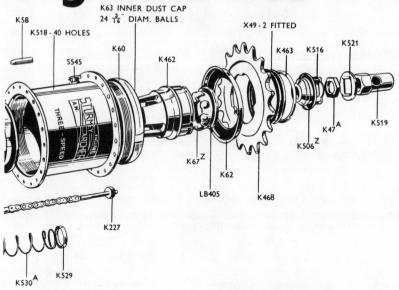

W. 3 SPEED HUB

K63 INNER DUST CAP
24 $\frac{3}{16}$" DIAM. BALLS

" long)	K462	Driver
	K67Z	Ball Cage with $\frac{1}{4}$" balls
	LB405	Outer Dust Cap
	K506Z	Axle Cone with Dust Cap
	K516	R.H. Cone Locking Washer
	K513	Low Gear Pawl
	K518	Shell, 40 holes
	S545	Lubricator
	K517	L.H. Ball Cup
	K504Z	Indicator
	K227	Connection Locknut
	X42A	Axle Spacing Washer ($\frac{1}{8}$" thick)
	K47A	Cone Locknut
	K521	Axle Washer
	K519	R.H. Axle Nut
	K520	L.H. Axle Nut
of 24)	K62	Sprocket Dust Cap
	K468	Sprocket 18 teeth
	X49	Sprocket Spacing Washer ($\frac{1}{16}$" thick)
	K463	Circlip

TRIGGER HANDLEBAR CONTROL

GC3B	Trigger control complete—less Pulley
GA244B	Trigger Unit complete
L52	Trigger Lever only
K730A	Pin for Trigger Lever
L53Z	Ratchet Plate
K731A	Pivot Pin
L55	Trigger Pawl
L56	Trigger Spring
X69	Clip Screw
X111A	Clip Nut
K739Z	Trigger Wire Assembly (Specify size)
	52½" × 17½" Boy's 21" Diamond frame Models
	55½" × 21½" Girl's 19" Parallel Tube Models
	Boy's 20" Triplex frame Models
	Girl's 19" Duplex frame Models
	Girl's 18" Curved Parallel Tube Models

K744	Fulcrum Sleeve
K745Z	Fulcrum clip complete 1" diam. for Diamond and Parallel Tube frames only
K745C	Fulcrum Clip complete 1⅛" diam. for Boy's Duplex and Triplex frames only
K745BZ	Fulcrum Clip complete 1⅛" diam. for Girl's Duplex frames only
X90	Clip Screw
X78BZ	Pulley complete for 1⅛" tube (all models)
X69	Clip Screw
X78	Pulley Wheel only
X79	Pulley Arm
X80	Pulley Arm Screw
X110B	Clip with Pulley Stud for 1⅛" tube
X109B	Half Clip for 1⅛" tube

The Sturmey Archer AW 3 speed gear.

To dis-mantle the AW hub, it's best to work on a fully equipped work— bench with a good vise. If you don't have one available, use a flat table.
1. Remove left-hand cone locknut(K520) and all washers(K521). When dismantling any mechanical unit, note the order you remove parts. If it's possible, place parts on table in order of their removal. This also gives you a chance to inspect individual parts for damage or wear.
2. Remove left-hand cone(K506Z).
3. Unscrew right-hand ball ring(K60) from hub shell. The unit is notched and you must break it loose with a hammer and punch. Remove the unit
4. The ball ring contains one notch with the letters SA engraved. Mark the nearest spoke to this notch with a piece of tape or string. When you re-assemble the unit the RH ball ring will be inserted nearest the mark- ed spoke. The right-hand ball ring has a two start thread and must be started in the exact spot, or the rear wheel will be out of alignment.
5. If the situation calls for removing the sprocket(K468) from the driver (K462), remove the holding clip(K463). Remove in order, spacing wash- ers(X49), the sprocket, and outer dust cap(K62).
    a. There must be two washers and they must be replaced in same position they were removed, in relation to sprocket offset, in order to maintain original chain line.
6. Remove low gear pawls, pins, and springs(K513).
7. If a vise is available, place left end of axle in it and remove right - hand locknut(K519), washer (K521), cone lock washer(K47A), and cone (K506Z).
8. Next pull off the clutch spring(K530A), the driver(K462), right ball ring(LB405), and gear ring(K511A).
9. Remove gear ring pawls(K512), pins, and springs(K58-K64).
10. Remove the thrust ring (K528A), washer (K411), and unscrew ind- icator rod(K504Z).
11. Tap out key(K526), and remove sliding clutch(K505A), and the sleeve (K527).
12. Remove planet cage (K515), and planet pinions (K16) and pin(K516)
13. If left bearing(K67Z) is worn, remove from the hub shell. It has a left-hand thread.
14. The dust caps in left ball cup and driver are pressed in at factory. If ball retainer must be replaced due to wear, replace dust cap also.
After the assembly has been dismantled, check additional points for worn or broken parts. The trouble spots are listed below.
1. Sliding clutch in driver. It must slide up and down easily.
2. Check the axle, it must be perfectly straight, and without marks.
3. Check gear teeth. If chipped or worn on peaks, replace the gear.
4. Check all raceways for wear. Replace if worn or pitted.
5. Check all pinion pins, sliding clutch, and gear ring splines for wear (rounding off) at all contact points.
6. Check pawls and pawl ratchets for wear.

How to re-assemble the Sturmey Archer AW 3 speed hub.

1. If the left-hand ball cup was removed from hub shell (K518), turn it back in place by screwing on counterclockwise.
2. Fit the pawls, pins, and springs back into gear ring(K511).
    a. Place gear ring, with teeth pointing down, on a flat surface.

b. Place a pawl spring along the side of a pawl, until the loop is over pin hole, and foot is under long nose of the pawl.

c. Hold pawl pin in left hand, grip nose of pawl and foot of spring between thumb and forefinger of your right hand and slide the pawl inside, tail first, between flanges of the gear ring. When the hole in the pawl, and loop of the spring, coincide with holes in the flange part, push the pawl spring into place.

3. Grease channels of dust caps of left-hand ball cup, driver and recess of right-hand ball ring only.

4. Hold left end of axle in the vise. Turn until slot for axle key is over sun pinion(see explanation of gear operation page 62).

a. Fit into planet cage.

b. Add the planet pinions and pins, with small ends of pins sticking out.

5. Fit the sleeve (flange first), sliding clutch with recess on flange of the sleeve, and axle key with flat portion facing up, and screw indicator rod in place to hold components in position.

6. Fit thrust ring and washer over flat ends of key, in place on slotted ring.

7. Slip gear ring unit in place.

8. Replace the right-hand ball ring and inner dust cap.

9. Place the driver and ball cage in proper position.

10. Clutch spring fits over axle.

11. Screw right-hand cone up finger tight, then back it off 1/2 turn and lock in place with a special washer and locknut.

a. Never back cone more than 1/2 turn. Over-adjustment could throw gear mechanism out of adjustment and cause serious damage.

12. Remove hub assembly from the vise and turn it over, with other end in the vise.

13. Fit planet cage pawls in place.

a. Place one pawl between the flanges with flat driving side pointing to the right.

b. Insert a pin pawl through outside flange and half-way through the pawl. Use tweezers and grip bent leg of pawl spring and pull spring along underside of pawl until the loop of the spring is in line with the hole through the pawl, and both legs of the spring are between the pawl and planet cage.

c. Push the pawl pin into place. Pawl should be pointing to right with driving edge pointing up.

14. Remove unit from the vise. Oil the planet cage before replacing on your bike.

15. Insert the unit into the hub shell and screw right-hand ball ring in (two-start right hand thread). Line mark etched SA with marked spoke when the two turns don't place the ball ring in correct position.

16. Fit left cone into place, add washers and locknut, the same order of removal in reverse, and adjust hub bearings.

17. If the sprocket was removed from the driver, fit outer dust cap over the driver before replacing sprocket. Center dust cap properly on the driver flange. Replace sprocket and spacing washers in correct order and add the retaining clip.

18. Replace wheel in cycle and make adjustment to gear if necessary.

a. Set control lever in center gear position(number two gear).

b. To adjust, loosen locknut on knurled connection rod.

c. Rotate connecting rod until end of indicator rod is even with the end of axle. Tighten the locknut.

How the Sturmey Archer 3 speed hub operates.

The use of the term planet wheel, etc. in service procedure and repairs is more than a coincidence. The SA 3 speed hub operates very much the same as our solar system.

Refer to figure 71, page 59, and notice the position of gears in the gear ring. The assembly is shown in simple form and consists of a central gear or pinion, around which rotates a similiar gear. The toothed gear ring surrounds both. The central gear, which doesn't rotate, is called the sun wheel. The gear which rolls between the sun wheel and gear ring is called the planet wheel.

Although the drawing illustrates only one planet gear, it's more practical if there are two, three or four gears. Sturmey Archer AW units have four. The four planet wheels carry the planet cage with them(figure 71, page 59), and provide a support for the planet wheel spindles.

The basic involved is simple. As the planet wheel rotates around the fixed sun wheel, the center of the planet wheel moves slower than the outer rim of the gear.

Refer once again to figure 71, page 59, and review the diagrams in fig. 2. One planet gear is shown for clarity. Assuming the sun wheel is securely fixed to the stationary axle, as in the Sturmey Archer assembly, the unit functions as follows:

A gear ring is attached to the drive sprocket of the axle and coupled to the hub shell (B). This is a direct drive from sprocket to the hub, and the planet pinions, while rotating around the central sun pinion, would not be working. That's exactly what happens when the bike is in 2nd gear(normal driving gear).

When the top gear is used, the planet spindle A, which is located in the planet cage, center of the planet gear, is connected to the drive sprocket and is moved toward the arrow, which causes the planet wheel to roll all around the sun wheel. As teeth mesh with teeth from inside the gear ring, it drives the gear ring at a faster speed. When the gear ring is connected to the hub shell, it turns the wheel at a faster rate and the bike is in high.

The last diagram illustrates the comparative position when unit is in low gear. The gear ring is connected to the drive sprocket, which drives the planet pinions together with the planet cage at a slower speed than the gear ring is moving. When planet cage is connected to the hub shell, low gear is engaged.

When the bike is in normal gear, drive is from sprocket direct to gear ring to the hub shell. Planet wheels rotate, without stress, around the sun wheel.

When bike is in top gear, drive is from sprocket to planet pinion spindle. Planet pinion rolls around the fixed sun pinion. Outer edge of planet pinion moves faster, drives the gear ring, which is connected to the hub shell.

When bike is in low gear, drive is from sprocket to gear ring. This rotates the planet pinions around the sun pinion. The planet pinion spindles move faster than the gear ring. Planet spindles are coupled via the planet-cage to the hub shell.

The gears are always in mesh and can't be damaged by incorrect gear changing. A four-prong clutch slides into engagement with ends of planet pins for the top gear, and to mesh with internal dogs or splines on the gear ring for other ratios. This component is coupled to the hub by the free-wheel pawls, which are located, one set in the gear ring, and the other in the planet cage. When bike is in low gear, the ends of the sliding clutch depress the ends of the pawls in the gear ring and hold them away from engaging the hub shell, directing the drive through the planet cage pawls.

Figure 72
Trigger control assembly for the Sturmey Archer 3 speed unit.

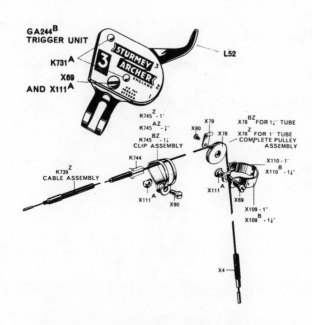

GA244^B TRIGGER UNIT
K731^A
X69
AND X111^A
L52
K745^Z - 1"
K745^{AZ} - $\frac{1}{2}$"
K745^{BZ} - 1$\frac{1}{4}$"
CLIP ASSEMBLY
X79
X80
X78
X78^{BZ} FOR 1$\frac{1}{4}$" TUBE
X78^Z FOR 1" TUBE
COMPLETE PULLEY ASSEMBLY
K744
K739^Z
CABLE ASSEMBLY
X111^A
X90
X111
X69
X110 - 1"
X110^B - 1$\frac{1}{4}$"
X109 - 1"
X109^B - 1$\frac{1}{4}$"
X4

Figure 73
The Sportshift 3 speed gear control assembly.

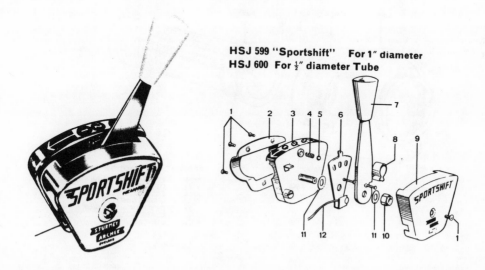

HSJ 599 "Sportshift"　For 1" diameter
HSJ 600 For $\frac{1}{2}$" diameter Tube

Figure 74
Sturmey Archer Auto Twist grip control- 3 speed

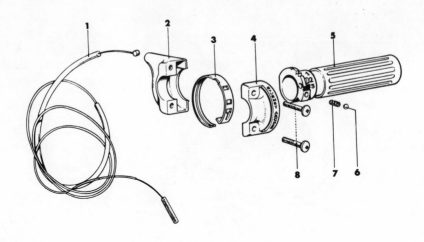

Figure 75
Twist control- old style.

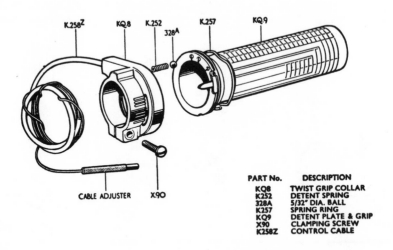

CABLE ADJUSTER   X90

PART No.	DESCRIPTION
KQ8	TWIST GRIP COLLAR
K252	DETENT SPRING
328A	5/32" DIA. BALL
K257	SPRING RING
KQ9	DETENT PLATE & GRIP
X90	CLAMPING SCREW
K258Z	CONTROL CABLE

Most control units operate in a similiar manner. The Sturmey Archer 3 speed control referred to on the previous pages can be serviced alike.
Figure 76

HSJ 583 Twist Grip complete with Cable and Spare Grip

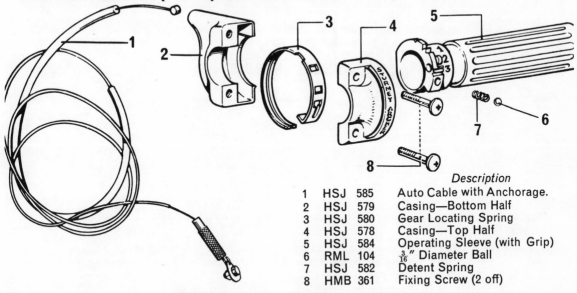

			Description
1	HSJ	585	Auto Cable with Anchorage.
2	HSJ	579	Casing—Bottom Half
3	HSJ	580	Gear Locating Spring
4	HSJ	578	Casing—Top Half
5	HSJ	584	Operating Sleeve (with Grip)
6	RML	104	$\frac{3}{16}$" Diameter Ball
7	HSJ	582	Detent Spring
8	HMB	361	Fixing Screw (2 off)

Cable fitting and gear setting.

1. Fit spring(7) and steel ball(3/16" in diameter) into recess cut in the handle grip.
2. Fit cable nipple into slotted recess of operating sleeve.
3. Fit cable inner wire into slot of gear locating spring(3), and position spring over operating sleeve. Be sure the steel ball is positioned in the elongated hole of the gear locating spring.
4. Keep your thumb over the ball, and spring, as you feed inner wire - into cable slot of bottom half of casing(2). Press spring into casing until the spring clicks down into the groove.
5. Fit upper portion of casing (4) over operating sleeve (5). Hold both halves of casing together and screw clamping screws into place.
6. Place grip control in place on handlebars.

    a. Slide the control up handlebar as far as it will go, and adjust the grip to proper position with gear numbers facing upward.

    b. Tighten both casing screws.

    c. Fit fulcrum clip on top tube of bike frame.

    d. Pass cable inner wire through fulcrum clip and feed wire cable into clip slot.

    e. Push outer cable up to fulcrum slot.

    f. Fit inner wire under pulley arm to pulley wheel.

    g. Connect control cable to gear indicator chain at rear wheel hub.

    h. Slide clip along upper frame and take out any slack in the control cable.

    i. Tighten fulcrum clip bolt securely.

If you have just purchased your bike the gear adjustment is probably in factory setting and will not require further adjustment. However, if you're buying the bike second hand, or converting to the three-speed unit, gear

Page 66

adjustment is probably needed. See figure 77 and the text following.

Figure 77

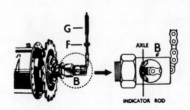

Gear Adjustment(old style grip control)

1. Place twist control gear indicator in number 2 position.
2. Screw cable connection adjuster(G) until the end of indicator rod is exactly level with extreme end of axle.
    a. Check the adjustment through window cut in nut(B).
3. Tighten locknut(F).
4. If you can't make enough adjustment in this manner, loosen screw holding fulcrum clip and move the clip until enough cable is present.

Cable.
    If it's necessary to remove control cable, remove the control from handlebars.
    1. Remove spring ring(use a screwdriver) from behind the collar
    2. Remove grip from collar and plate. Don't lose ball or spring.
    3. To replace a cable, place collar face down on a table.
    4. Fit nipple of new cable into the recess.
        a. Fit inner wire into groove around the edge of the plate.
    5. Place spring and ball into place. Dab on a little grease.
    6. Follow steps on page 65 to replace the unit.
    7. Lubricate twist control frequently with oil in indicator slot.

Gear adjustment for new style unit(figure 76).

    1. Connect control cable to gear indicator chain at rear hub.
    2. Slide fulcrum clip along frame to remove excess slack.
    3. Twist grip control until bottom gear(1), low gear, is indicated.
        a. Blue section will be visible through opening. Keep handle moving until no movement is possible. Gear should be adjusted.
    4. Screw gear indicator locknut up to cable and tighten.
    5. If adjustment is incorrect, and no color is visible through the opening, all adjustment has been used.
        a. Dismantle the twist control and refit the indicator spring unit.

The next several pages deal with the service and adjustment of the five speed gear unit. Although control service tips are getting the cart before the horse, they do fit in with the three speed control service tip section.

Assembly.

1. Loosen screws holding support plate and remove plate from control.
2. Push small lever to backward position.
3. Bring out as much cable (inner wire) as possible of left unit. Push inner wire, from back of control, through opening at top of control and insert nipple into recess at base of lever.
4. Curve inner wire around base of lever and push outer cable stop into the slot at the side of the control.
5. Replace the plate.
6. Remove right cover plate.
7. Push right control lever to central position.
8. Insert larger cable nipple into recess at base of the lever.
9. Push wire through slot of cable anchor spot.
10. Push outer cable up to anchor spot.

Place the unit on your bike. On boys bike, 3" from frame lug to front edge of support plate. On girls bike, 1 1/2" from frame lug.

Be sure the rear brake cable fits in recess in "Twinshift" back plate, before fitting support plate to the frame tube.

(GC5A) DUAL CONTROL

"TWINSHIFT" GEAR CONTROL

		LEFT	RIGHT			LEFT	RIGHT	
	1st GEAR SUPER LOW	Backward	Backward	1st GEAR SUPER LOW		Backward	Backward	
	2nd GEAR LOW	Forward	Backward	2nd GEAR LOW		Forward	Backward	
	3rd GEAR NORMAL – i.e. (Direct Drive)	Forward	Central	3rd GEAR NORMAL – i.e. (Direct Drive)		Forward	Central	
	4th GEAR HIGH	Forward	Forward	4th GEAR HIGH		Forward	Forward	
	5th GEAR SUPER HIGH	Backward	Forward	5th GEAR SUPER HIGH		Backward	Forward	

The terms left and right and forward or backward refer to the rider's position when seated on bicycle.

Sturmey Archer S5, the five speed hub gear unit.

Figure 79

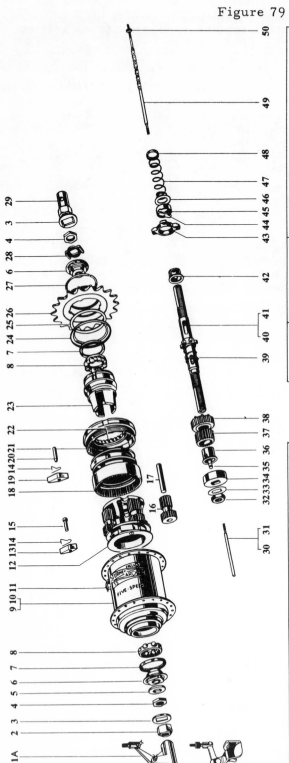

PHOTO No.	SALES No.	DESCRIPTION
26	HSL 716-720	Sprocket – 16-20T
27	HSL 721	Sprocket Circlip
28	HMW 147	Cone Lockwasher
29	HMN 129	Right-hand Axle Nut
30	HSA 266	Gear Push Rod (6″ Axle)
31	HSA 267	Gear Push Rod (6¼″ Axle)
32	HMN 133	Locknut for Dog-Ring
33	HMW 149	Lockwasher for Dog-Ring
34	HSA 138	Dog-Ring
35	HSA 268	Low Gear Axle Key
36	HSA 140	Pinion Sleeve
37	HSA 141	Secondary Sun Pinion
38	HSA 269	Primary Sun Pinion
39	HSA 273	Low Gear Spring
40	HSA 274	Axle – 6″
41	HSA 145	Axle – 6¼″
42	HSA 116	Clutch Sleeve
43	HSA 117	Clutch
44	HSA 124	Axle Key
45	HSA 127	Thrust Ring
46	HMW 148	Thrust Washer
47	HSA 128	Clutch Spring
48	HSA 129	Spring Cap
49	HSA 126	Gear Indicator Rod Right-hand (6″ Axle)
	HSA 126	Gear Indicator Rod Right-hand (6¼″ Axle)
50	HMN 134	Connector Locknut

PHOTO No.	SALES No.	DESCRIPTION
1	HSJ 608	Bellcrank (Steel)
1A	HSJ 606	Bellcrank (Plastic)
2	HMN 128	Left-hand Axle Nut
3	HMW 145	Axle Washer
4	HMN 132	Locknut
5	HMW 129	Axle Spacing Washer (⅛″)
6	HSA 101	Cone
7	HSA 102	Outer Dust Cap
8	HSA 103	Ball Cage
9	HSA 271	Shell – 40 Hole – and Ball Cup Combined
10	HSA 270	Shell – 36 Hole – and Ball Cup Combined
11	HSA 106	Lubricator (Plastic)
12	HSA 132	Planet Cage
13	HSA 111	Low Gear Pawl
14	HSA 120	Pawl Spring
15	HSA 133	Pawl Pin – Planet Cage
16	HSA 134	Planet Pinion
17	HSA 135	Pinion Pin
18	HSA 118	Gear Ring
19	HSA 119	Gear Ring Pawl
20	HSA 112	Pawl Pin – Gear Ring
21	HSA 121	Right-hand Ball Ring
22	HSA 122	Inner Dust Cap
23	HSA 123	Driver
24	HSL 701	Sprocket Dust Cap
25	HMW 127	Sprocket Spacing Washer

Dis-mantling the S5 Sturmey Archer hub.

1. Remove the left cone locknut(4), washers(3), and lay them out in the order they will be replaced on the unit.
2. Mark right ball ring and shell before removal. Ball ring has a two-start thread, and marks must match when reassembled.
3. Remove right ball ring(2) from the hub shell. Use hammer and the punch method, hit one of the notches, and withdraw components as unit.
4. Place left end of axle in a vise and remove the right-hand locknut(29) and washers(3), cone washers(4), and right-hand cone(6).
5. Remove in order, the clutch spring(47), and cap(48), the driver(23), right-hand ball ring(8), and the gear ring(18).
6. Remove the thrust washer(46), and ring(45).
7. Push the axle key out of place and remove clutch sleeve(42), and the sliding clutch(43).
8. Push out all pinion pins and remove pinions and planet cage(12).
9. Low gear pawl pins are riveted in place. If it's necessary to remove them, file the rivet flat and knock the pins out with a small punch and hammer. Remove the pawls and pawl springs.
10. Place right end of axle in the vise.
11. Straighten edges of the tab washer before removing nut(32), and tab washer (33) holding the internally toothed dog ring, and remove the dog ring(34).
12. Push both sun pinions along the axle until the larger one engages the axle dogs. Move sleeve under the smaller one in the opposite direction until the second axle key(35), is exposed. Remove the key(35).
13. Slide both sun pinions(37 & 38), sleeve(36), and spring off the axle.
14. If it's necessary to remove dust caps from driver and left-hand ball cup, pry it out carefully with a screwdriver. They are pressed in place at the factory. If you replace the ball retainers, replace the dust cap. After the unit is dismantled, check the following problem spots for any additional, or potential, trouble.
1. Slide clutch(43) up and down driver prongs(23). Movement must be completely free.
2. Examine gear rings for cracks, chips, or signs of internal wear.
3. Check axle for straightness.
4. Check all ball races for signs of wear.
5. Check sliding clutch for wear at points of engagement.
6. Examine all pinion teeth for signs of wear or breakage.
7. Check planet cage dogs for signs of excess wear.
8. Examine pawls and pawl ratchets for signs of wear.
9. Check axle dogs thoroughly. If worn, even slightly, replace them.

Figure 80

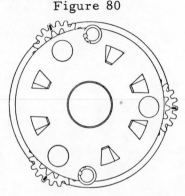

Re-assembly-S5

The easiest method of putting the S5 unit back together is to first prepare several sub-assemblies.

1. Fit the ball cage(8) into the left-hand ball cup(7), and shell assembly (9), with ring of the ball retainer facing outward. Recess of dust cap must also face outward. If you replaced the ball bearing cage, you must also replace the dust cap.

2. Place the ball cage into the driver with ring of the ball retainer facing outward. If a new ball retainer is used, replace the dust cover. If the sprocket has been removed from the driver, fit the outer dust cap over the driver before replacing the sprocket. Dust cap must be centered on the driver flange. Place sprocket and spacing washers in order of their removal. Add retaining clip(27).

3. Fit the balls and the inner dust cap to the right-hand ball ring and be certain the balls turn freely when dust cap is in place.

4. Place the pawls(19), pins(14), and springs in the gear ring(18).

5. Place gear ring, with teeth pointing down, on a flat surface. Place pawl spring alongside a pawl with loop over pin hole, and the foot under long nose of the pawl. Hold the pawl pin in your left hand, grip the nose of the pawl, and the foot of the spring between your thumb and forefinger of your right hand and slide the pawl, tail first, between the flanges of the gear ring. When the hole in the pawl and the loop of the spring coincide with holes in the flanges, push the pawl spring into place.

6. Fit the pawls, pins, and springs into the planet cage(12).

7. Hold the planet cage in your left hand, with flanges where the pawls are placed, away from you. Place one pawl between the flanges, with flat top surface pointing to the right, with hole in the pawl to the left of the holes in the flanges. Push a pawl pin through the hole in the inner flange and your left thumb over the pin head, hold it in contact with side of the pawl. Use your right hand and place the foot of pawl between the thumb and forefinger. Thread the straight leg under the pawl pin from the rear and pull forward until the loop of the spring encircles the pawl pin.

8. Use one of your right fingers to hold the foot of the spring under the nose of the pawl. With a finger of the left hand, move the pawl until the hole is aligned with holes in the flanges.
   a. Push pawl pin into place.

9. Grease should be placed in dust caps covering ball bearings ONLY No grease should be used in any other part of the gear hub.

When sub-assemblies are completed, assemble balance of the unit.

1. Slide low gear spring, primary sun pinion, and secondary sun pinion, and sleeve, onto the axle from the left side. Move into position until the dogs engage.

2. Hold pinions in place, withdraw the secondary sun pinion sleeve until low gear keyhole is exposed, and insert the low gear key. Be sure the keyhole is aligned with bore of the axle.
   a. Release the pinions. They should spring into place and secure the key.

3. Screw gear push rod into the low gear key.

4. Assemble dog ring until it engages the axle square. Secure with a washer and nut. Tighten securely. Turn edge of lock washer over two opposite sides of locknut to hold locknut securely in place.

5. Secure axle in a vise in a vertical position, and slide planet cage in position.

6. Add the double planet pinions and pins until they engage the two sun pinions.

7. Marked teeth must point radially outward. If they don't, hub will not be timed correctly.

    a. Notice that three teeth on the small end of each planet pinion are visible over the edge of the planet cage. To verify timing, engage the gear ring with the pinions and rotate to test.

    b. The unit must move freely.

8. Place clutch sleeve in place, flange first, sliding clutch with recess over flange of the sleeve, key, and thrust ring and washer. The notches of the thrust ring must engage flat side of the key.

9. Remove the axle from vise and insert indicator chain with coupling into the right end. Thread into axle key. Sliding clutch must be free to move along the axle until indicator chain is moved up and down.

10. Place gear ring, right-hand ball ring, driver, clutch spring and the clutch spring cap, in unit in proper order.

11. Place right-hand cone in place and turn down finger tight. Back off 1/2 turn and lock in place with lock washer and locknut. Don't turn it back more than 1/2 turn.

12. Place assembled unit into hub shell and screw right-hand ball ring up, finger tight.

13. Re-check marks on the ball ring and hub flange. If they match, go ahead and screw the ball ring up tightly. Tap with punch and hammer,

14. Fit left cone, washer, and locknut into place. Adjust hub bearing. When replacing the unit be certain the gear hub axle doesn't turn in the chainstay slots. The flat side of the axle should fit into frame. If the forks have been spread and won't hold the axle properly, refer to frame service in a previous chapter, and force fork ends closer together.

Gear Ratio on the S5 Sturmey Archer five speed hub.

    1. 5th gear(super high speed), 50% increase.
    2. 4th gear(high gear), 26.6% increase.
    3. Normal running gear, direct drive, 0% increase.
    4. Low gear, decrease 21.1%
    5. Super low gear, 33.3% decrease.

Gear adjustment for bikes with Twinshift, or GC5A dual control units.

    1. For right-hand side. Figure 81, page 72.

        a. Disconnect gear control cable by unscrewing adjuster(1).

        b. Screw chain guide(3) until it's flush with axle nut(4).

        c. Re-connect control cable.

    2. To adjust hub gear, set right control lever in central position and locknut(2), down.

        a. Observe chain through window in chain guide and screw cable adjuster(1) down until the last link of chain is clear of the axle.

        b. Adjust cable until end of rod is exactly even with outside of the axle. See figure B.

    3. For left side control.

        a. Remove bellcrank and locknut(Figure D), from rear frame, and fit bellcrank(3) up to left axle nut(5), and lock it in place on the axle with locknut(4).

        b. Screw locknut(2) down completely.

c. Push hand lever to forward position and screw cable connector to bell crank. Turn several turns.

d. Push lever to back position and screw cable connector until all play in the cable is gone.

e. Apply light pressure and push bell crank arm forward. Turn the wheel backward at the same time. If gears aren't fully engaged, move the bell crank arm forward more. Adjust as needed.

f. Screw cable connector up completely and tighten the locknut.

Figure 81

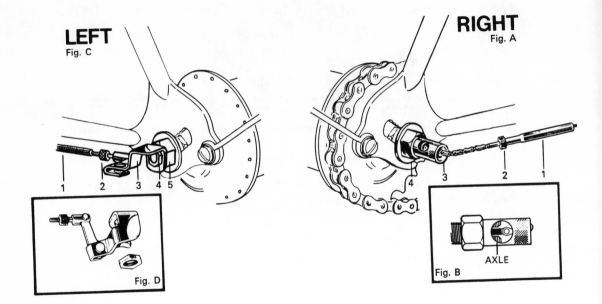

Figure 82
Gear ratio table for the S5 Sturmey Archer five speed gear.

NUMBER OF TEETH		26" WHEEL					27" WHEEL					28" WHEEL				
CHAINWHEEL	SPROCKET	1 SUPER LOW	2 LOW	3 NORMAL	4 HIGH	5 SUPER HIGH	1 SUPER LOW	2 LOW	3 NORMAL	4 HIGH	5 SUPER HIGH	1 SUPER LOW	2 LOW	3 NORMAL	4 HIGH	5 SUPER HIGH
40	14	49.5	58.7	74.3	94.1	111.5	51.4	61.0	77.1	97.7	115.7	53.3	63.2	80.0	101.3	120.0
	15	46.2	54.7	69.3	87.7	104.0	48.0	56.9	72.0	91.2	108.0	49.8	59.0	74.7	94.6	112.1
	16	43.3	51.3	65.0	82.3	97.5	45.0	53.3	67.5	85.4	101.3	46.7	55.3	70.0	88.6	105.0
	17	40.8	48.3	61.2	77.5	91.8	42.3	50.2	63.5	80.4	95.3	43.9	52.1	65.9	83.4	98.9
	18	38.5	45.7	57.8	73.2	86.7	40.0	47.4	60.0	76.0	90.0	41.5	49.1	62.2	78.7	93.3
	19	36.5	43.2	54.7	69.2	82.1	37.9	44.9	56.8	71.9	85.2	39.3	46.5	58.9	74.6	68.4
	20	34.7	41.1	52.0	65.8	78.0	36.0	42.7	54.0	68.4	81.0	37.3	44.2	56.0	70.9	84.0
	22	31.5	37.4	47.3	59.9	71.0	32.7	38.8	49.1	62.2	73.7	33.9	40.2	50.9	64.4	76.4
44	14	54.4	64.5	81.7	103.5	122.6	56.5	66.1	84.9	107.5	127.4	58.6	69.5	88.0	111.4	132.0
	15	50.8	60.3	76.3	96.6	114.5	52.7	62.6	79.2	100.2	118.8	54.7	64.9	82.1	104.0	123.2
	16	47.7	56.5	71.5	90.5	107.3	49.5	58.6	74.2	93.9	111.3	51.3	60.8	77.0	91.8	115.5
	17	44.9	53.2	67.3	85.2	100.6	46.6	55.2	69.9	88.4	104.9	48.3	57.3	72.5	86.6	108.8
	18	42.4	50.2	63.6	80.5	95.4	44.0	52.1	66.0	83.5	99.0	45.6	54.0	68.4	86.6	102.6
	19	40.1	47.6	60.2	76.2	90.3	41.7	49.4	62.5	79.1	93.8	43.2	51.2	64.8	82.0	97.2
	20	38.1	45.2	57.2	72.4	85.8	39.6	46.9	59.4	75.2	89.1	41.1	48.6	61.6	78.0	92.4
	22	34.7	41.1	52.0	65.8	78.0	36.0	42.7	54.0	68.4	81.0	37.3	44.2	56.0	70.9	84.0
46	14	56.9	67.5	85.4	108.1	128.1	59.1	70.1	88.7	112.3	133.1	61.3	72.7	92.0	116.5	138.0
	15	53.1	63.0	79.7	100.9	119.6	55.1	65.4	82.8	104.8	124.2	57.2	67.9	85.9	108.7	128.9
	16	49.8	59.0	74.4	94.5	112.1	51.7	61.3	77.6	98.2	116.4	53.7	63.6	80.5	101.9	120.8
	17	46.9	55.5	70.3	89.0	105.5	48.7	57.7	73.0	92.4	109.5	50.5	59.9	75.8	95.9	113.7
	18	44.3	52.5	66.4	84.0	99.6	46.0	54.5	69.0	87.3	103.5	47.7	56.5	71.5	90.5	107.3
	19	41.9	49.7	62.9	79.6	94.4	43.6	51.7	65.4	82.8	98.1	45.2	53.6	67.8	85.8	101.7
	20	39.9	47.2	59.8	75.7	89.7	41.4	49.1	62.1	78.6	93.2	42.9	50.9	64.4	81.5	96.6
	22	36.3	43.1	54.5	69.0	81.8	37.7	44.6	56.5	71.5	84.6	39.1	46.3	58.6	74.2	87.9
48	14	59.3	70.4	89.1	112.8	133.7	61.7	73.1	92.6	117.2	139.0	64.0	75.8	96.0	121.5	144.0
	15	55.4	65.7	83.2	105.3	124.8	57.5	68.3	86.4	109.4	129.6	59.7	70.8	89.6	113.4	134.4
	16	52.0	61.6	78.0	98.7	117.0	54.0	64.0	81.0	102.5	121.5	56.0	66.4	84.0	106.3	126.0
	17	49.0	58.0	73.5	93.0	110.3	50.8	60.2	76.2	96.4	114.3	52.7	62.5	79.1	100.2	118.7
	18	46.2	54.7	69.3	87.7	104.0	48.0	56.9	72.0	91.1	108.0	49.8	59.0	74.7	94.6	112.1
	19	43.8	51.9	65.7	83.2	98.6	45.5	53.9	68.2	86.3	102.5	47.1	55.8	70.7	89.5	106.1
	20	41.6	49.3	62.4	79.0	93.6	43.2	51.2	64.8	82.0	97.2	44.8	53.1	67.2	85.0	100.8
	22	37.8	44.8	56.7	71.8	85.1	39.3	46.6	58.9	74.5	88.4	40.7	48.3	61.1	77.3	91.7

Chapter Eight

Multi-gear units.

The latest version of a derailleur gear, the Allvit, by Huret, is a prime example of advancement in the cycling field.

Unlike many contemporary units employing the delailleur concept, the Allvit cage rises or falls as it's changed. The cage follows the contour of the freewheel block as it rises to engage the smaller sprockets, or falls to cope with the larger cogs. The guide roller and chain guide are always in an effective position to insure a smooth, troublefree gear change, secondly, the lowered position of the chain cage in low gear reduces the possibility of fouling spokes. The chain fully envelopes the sprocket, almost like the single gear bike, and makes it almost impossible for the chain to jump or slip from any of the gears.

This system does not employ an automatic chain tensioner and yet the tension remains almost constant on all gear ratios, through smooth gear changes.

Figure 83

A typical multi-gear sprocket unit.

Adjusting the Derailleur.

The unit can be placed on most bikes equipped with 3, 4 or 5 speed free-wheel units.
1. After placing the gear on the wheel, replace the wheel and mount the chain over the two rollers, onto the small freewheel sprocket and large chain ring. Figure 3, figure 84.
2. Adjust the outward movement position with screw(F), figure 3, fig. 84, with chain on small freewheel sprocket.
3. Fit the transmission with the control lever in forward position, and take up all slack in the cable without causing tension on the mechanism allowing cable a straight forward movement(C) figure 2, figure 84.
    a. After cable is properly adjusted, tighten cable clamp nut.
4. Use control lever and move chain to the large freewheel sprocket.
5. Adjust screw(E) figure 3, figure 84, until upward movement of the mechanism will not allow chain to ride over the large sprocket into the spokes.
6. You will notice that gear movement follows increasing diameter of the freewheel sprocket(B) figure 1, figure 84, in order to obtain a maximum wrap around of chain(D), thereby avoiding the risk of fouling the chain while the lowered position of the chain cage is in bottom gear(A).
7. When you've attained proper cable tension, cut excess cable from near the cable clamp.
8. Chain tension is regulated by placing the terminal spring loop in one of four tension slots on the outer cage plate(K), figure 3, figure 84.
9. As the unit wears, either cable stretching, chain loosening, or whatever, it is adjustable.

Figure 84

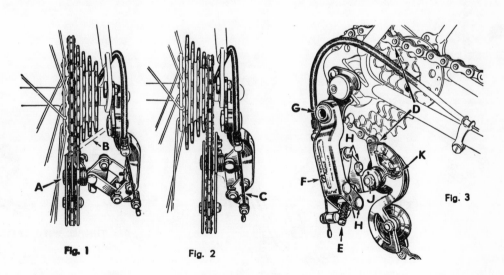

Fig. 1   Fig. 2   Fig. 3

Parts breakdown of the Huret "Allvit" gear ensemble.
Figure 85

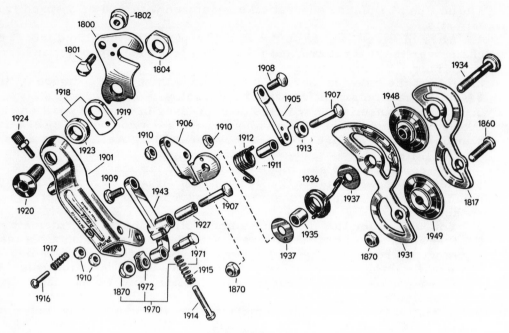

Figure 86
"Allvit" double control lever parts breakdown.

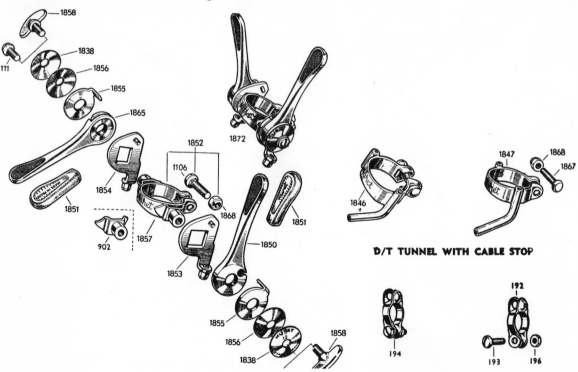

D/T TUNNEL WITH CABLE STOP

Shimano 5 speed derailleur parts breakdown.
Figure 87

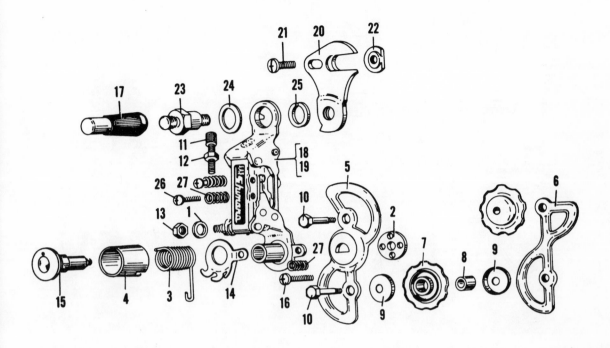

Figure 88
Shimano lark 5 speed derailleur parts breakdown.

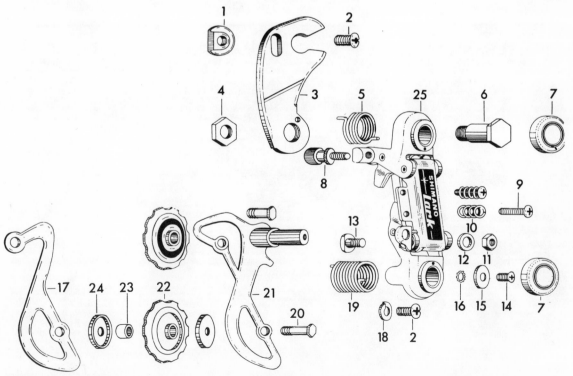

Figure 89
Shimano 3 & 5 speed Click-stick control assembly.

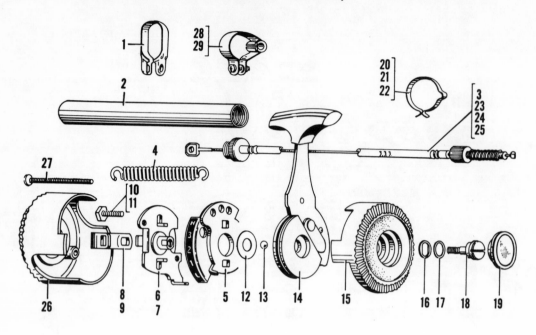

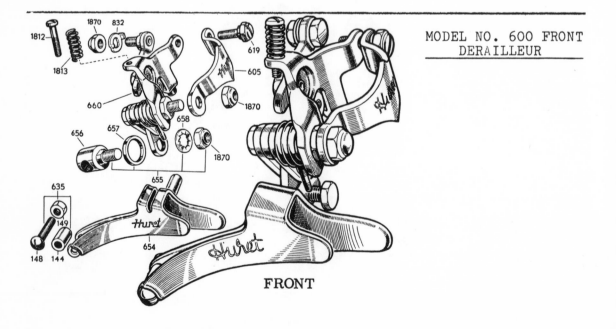

MODEL NO. 600 FRONT
DERAILLEUR

FRONT

Adjusting the Benelux series -multi-gears.

1. Lateral adjustment. Figure 90.
   a. Line up jockey sprocket(9T) with low gear.
   b. Loosen locknut(OE62), and adjust knurled head(OE60) of adjusting sleeve.
   c. Derailling cage must be parallel with freewheel.
   d. Tension the gear with knurled cap(B16). Ease it away from the hexagon part and turn clockwise as needed.
2. Cable fitting.
   a. Set in low gear position.
   b. Toggle chain must be free to rotate.
   c. To avoid over shooting low gear sprocket, inner cable must not be tight when assembled to toggle chain.

Figure 90

Figure 91

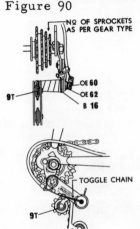

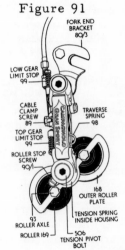

Adjusting the Campagnolo gear.

1. Lateral adjustment. Figure 91
   a. Adjust top limit stop(99), until chain rollers(169) are vertically in line with high speed gear sprocket.
   b. Move linkage over and align rollers(169) with bottom gear. It is adjusted by moving bottom limit stop(99).
2. To adjust the chain, first be certain upper chain roller is in contact with the chain, when chain is in contact with largest sprocket.
   a. Also largest chainwheel if double chainwheel is used.
   b. To adjust chain tension, unscrew roller axle(93) and remove the bottom roller, which frees chain from the roller cage.
   c. Unscrew peg stop(90/1) which allows roller cage to unwind.
   d. Unscrew main tension pivot bolt(506).
   e. Fit end of tension spring into proper hole in outer roller plate.
   f. Turn roller cage until twin roller plates are the bottom position and re-tighten peg stop.
   g. Fit chain and roller into position in roller cage.
   h. Tighten roller axle.
3. Proper alignment of the chain.
   a. On bike equipped with 5 speed gear, single chainwheel, chainwheel must be in line with middle sprocket.
   b. When the double chainwheel is used, proper alignment is made when chain-line is centered between chainwheels and center gear.

Adjusting the Benelux Super 60.

1. Lateral adjustment. Figure 92.
    a. Align the 9-tooth jockey sprocket with top gear sprocket.
    b. Loosen lower stroke adjusting screw(CY 38), adjust as needed.
2. Chain adjustment.
    a. Fit chain into derailling cage.
    b. Derail chain onto low gear and position properly by adjusting a upper stroke adjusting screw.
    c. Set angular position of gear by adjusting stop(CY60), in elong- ated slot in stop plate(CY30).
    d. Adjust until chain gives one complete link(3 rivets) from where chain leaves low gear sprocket to point of meeting jockey sprocket gear.
    e. Derail chain back to top gear to double check maximum wrap a- round of chain on all sprockets.
    f. If necessary, add a link of chain, or change angular position of adjusted gear until transition is smooth.
3. Tension adjustment.
    a. Radial tension of the derailling cage is adjusted with screw(52), figure 92. Don't remove screw completely.
    b. If derailling action to top gear is slow, tension is too light.
    c. Remove leg of arm return spring(CY34), from rear link(CY22).
    d. Remove retaining clip from spring tension shaft(CY48).
    e. Withdraw shaft until the notch clears the peg.
    f. Turn shaft clockwise until next notch catches the peg.
    g. Replace the spring and retaining clip.
    h. If the control cable breaks, it's still possible to ride your bike in one gear. Mount chain on sprocket and set lower adjusting con- trol screw as needed to hold the adjustment.

Figure 92

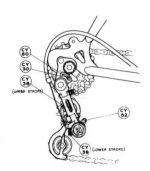
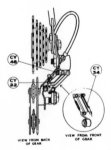

Chapter Nine

Troubleshooting and safety tips.

This chapter on troubleshooting will review, in capsule form, some of repair methods found throughout the book.

The front wheel and tire.

If the front wheel wobbles.
1. The wheel may be loose.   1. Tighten both axle nuts.
2. Cones may be worn.   2. Adjust as needed.
3. Hub may be cracked.   3. Replace the hub.
4. Bearings may be worn.   4. Replace the bearings.

If the wheel rubs against the fork.
1. Wheel is not centered properly 1. Loosen axle nuts and center.
2. Fork legs may be bent.   2. Straighten forks as needed.

If the wheel turns slowly.
1. Cones may be too tight.   1. Loosen one side and adjust cone.
2. Bearings may be frozen.   2. Grease, or replace if badly worn.
3. Axle may be broken.   3. Replace broken axle.

Spoke service tips.
1. Spoke missing.   1. See page 22.
   a. When replacing a spoke remember, one spoke goes down in hub
   and the next comes up through the hub.
   b. Every other spoke goes down, and every other one comes up.
2. Spoke is loose.   2. Tighten loose spokes firmly.
3. Spoke is loose, several.   3. Tighten all spokes equally well.
   a. It's a good idea to use a spoke straightening tool.
   b. Always start at valve hole and go around clockwise.
4. Test spoke tightness.   4. Pluck like a guitar string.
   a. If it's too tight, the spoke will make a sharp ping.
   b. If it's too loose, the spoke will make a dull thud noise.
5. To completely re-spoke a wheel, turn to page 22 and follow the general instructions from that text.

Flat tire.
1. Tube is punctured.   1. Repair as needed.
2. Tire is ripped.   2. If not too bad, repair with a boot.

2. Tire keeps losing air.
    a. Check the valve stem.   a. If spring is loose, tighten it.
    b. Valve stem broken.   b. If broken, replace it.

Rear Wheel.

Wheel turns hard.
    a. Axle nuts may be too tight.   a. Loosen axle locknuts.
    b. Bearings may be worn.   b. Replace the bearings.
    c. Wheel may be rubbing fork.   c. Center wheel and tighten locknuts.

Chain keeps jumping off the sprocket.
    a. Chain too loose.   a. Should have 1/2" play at center.
    b. Broken roller links.   b. Replace them.
    c. Crank sprocket is worn.   c. Replace it.
    d. Crank sprocket is crooked.   d. If slight, straighten it.

Coaster Brake.

If the brake works loose.
    a. Arm comes loose from clip.   a. Loosen rear nut and turn arm for-
                                         ward to tighten the brake.
    b. Brake clip breaks.   b. Replace and fasten to the frame.
    c. Coasting is lazy/brake drags. c. Grease the unit as needed.
    d. Grinding noise from hub.   d. Replace the bearings.
    e. Wheel slips constantly.   e. Replace worn clutch.
    f. Brakes grab.   f. Oil the hub assembly.
    g. Bike is hard to pump.   g. Brake discs probably sticking to-
                                         gether if New Departure unit.

Three speed coaster brake-Sturmey Archer.

No low gear.
    a. Low gear pawl upside down.   a. Re-assemble pawls correctly.
    b. Pawls pointing wrong way.   b. Re-assemble pawls correctly.
    c. Sliding clutch thrust collar not
        seating over axle key.   c. Fit thrust collar correctly.
    d. Incorrect axle spring.   d. Fit correct axle spring.

Slipping in low gear(1st).
    a. Sliding clutch nosed off, due
        to bad adjustment.   a. Fit new clutch and adjust right.
    b. Indicator not screwed home. b. Screw indicator up firmly.
    c. Right cone wrongly adjusted c. Re-adjust cone correctly.
    d. Bad trigger cable ends, or it
        has kinks in trigger wire.   d. Fit new cable control.
    e. Twisted indicator chain.   e. Replace and don't over-tighten.

Fluctuating between low gear(1st) and normal(2nd).
    a. Faulty or worn gear ring pawl. a. Change both gear ring pawls.

Slipping in normal gear(2nd).
    a. Gear ring dogs and/or sliding
        clutch nosed off.   a. Fit new gear ring and clutch.
    b. Indicator not screwed up tight. b. Screw indicator up firmly.

Slipping in top gear(3rd)
    a. Pinion pins or clutch worn. a. Replace parts and adjust with care.

b. Weak or distorted axle spring. b. Fit new spring in place.
c. Incorrect R. H. cone adjustment.
                                                      c. Re-adjust cone as needed.
d. Grit in clutch sleeve and axle. d. Clean the area thoroughly.

Hub turns stiffly. Drag on pedals when free-wheeling.
  a. Too many balls in ball ring. a. Only 24 balls should be used.
  b. Cones too tight. b. Re-adjust the cones.
  c. Chainstay ends not parallel. c. Correct chainstay ends. The ends must be parallel or axle will be under strain and subject to damage.
  d. Corrosion due to lack of oil. d. Oil the hub with a good oil.
  e. Distorted dust caps. e. Replace distorted caps.

Sluggish gear change.
  a. Distorted axle spring. a. Replace the spring.
  b. Bent axle. b. Replace the axle at once.
  c. Worn toggle chain link. c. Replace indicator and chain
  d. Guide pulley out of line d. Correct alignment of pulley on the frame.
  e. Flick control not oiled. e. Lubricate the control as needed.
  f. Control wire frayed. f. Replace control wire.
  g. Loose parts in unit. g. Check all components.

The brake. Noisy or shuddering brake.
  a. Loose brake arm clip. a. Tighten clip nuts and bolts.

Brake catchs, or grabs.
  a. Lack of oil. a. Lubricate through hole in hub.

The AW three speed gear.
No low gear.
  a. Low gear pawls upside down. a. Re-assemble correctly.
  b. Collar not seating over key. b. Fit correctly.
  c. Incorrect axle spring. c. Replace with proper part.

Slipping in low gear.
  a. Sliding clutch worn. a. Replace with proper part.
  b. Indicator not screwed up tight. b. Re-adjust as needed.
  c. RH cone adjusted wrong. c. Re-adjust as needed.
  d. Kinks in trigger wire. d. Replace the wire.
  e. Twisted indicator chain. e. Replace the chain.

Fluctuating between first and second gear.
  a. Worn gear ring pawls. a. Replace the pawls.

Slipping in second gear.
  a. Gear ring dogs/clutch worn. a. Replace worn parts as needed.
  b. Indicator not screwed up tight. b. Re-adjust as needed.

Slipping in top gear.
  a. Pinion pins/clutch worn. a. Replace as needed.
  b. Weak or distorted axle spring. b. Fit new spring in place.
  c. Incorrect cone(RH) adjusting. c. Re-adjust RH cone only.
  d. Grit in clutch sleeve or axle. d. Clean thoroughly.

Hub turns stiffly. Drag on pedals.
- a. Too many balls in ball ring.
- b. Cones adjusted to tightly.
- c. Chainstay ends not parallel.
- d. Corrosion in hub-lack of oil.
- e. Distorted dust caps.

- a. There should be only 24.
- b. Re-adjust as needed.
- c. Correct as needed.
- d. Oil hub using a high quality oil.
- e. Replace as needed.

Sluggish gear change.
- a. Distorted axle spring.
- b. Bent axle.
- c. Worn toggle chain link.
- d. Guide pulley out of line.
- e. Lack of oil
- f. Frayed control wire.

- a. Replace the springs.
- b. Replace if unable to straighten.
- c. Replace as needed.
- d. Re-align properly.
- e. Oil properly.
- f. Replace the wire.

Sturmey Archer S5 five speed gear.

No super low gear.
- a. Control cable(left) too slack.
- b. Low gear pawl upside down.

- a. Tighten control cable.
- b. Re-assemble low gear pawls.

Difficulty in engaging gears 1 & 2.
- a. Inner wired cable not lubed.
- b. Distorted low gear spring.
- c. Axle key bent.

- a. Lubricate with a good oil.
- b. Fit in a new spring.
- c. Replace. Don't try to straighten.

Slipping in low gear(1).
- a. Kinks in gear cables
- b. Faulty coiling-low gear spring
- c. Pawl springs in wrong.

- a. Fit new control cable.
- b. Replace the spring.
- c. Fit pawl springs properly.

Alternates between super low(1) or low(2) and normal gear(3).
- a. Faulty gear ring pawls.

- a. Replace the gear ring pawls.

Slips in low(2) and super low gear(1).
- a. Log ring locknut loose.
- b. Weak low gear spring.
- c. Dog ring teeth worn.

- a. Examine dogs for damage.
- b. Replace the spring.
- c. Replace the dog ring.

Slips in low(2) and high(4) gears.
- a. Overtight cable(left side).

- a. Loosen cable connector at hub.

Slips in normal gear(3).
- a. Gear ring/sliding clutch worn.

- a. Replace and check adjustment.

Slips in high(4) and super high gear(5).
- a. Planet cage dogs/clutch worn.
- b. Incorrect RH cone adjustment.
- c. Tight clutch spring/ or dirty.

- a. Replace parts, check clutch spring.
- b. Re-adjust properly.
- c. Replace spring or clean the hub.

Hub runs stiffly. Drag on pedal when free-wheeling.
- a. Planet pinions out of time.
- b. Too many balls in ball ring.
- c. Bad cone adjustment.
- d. Chainstay ends not parallel.
- e. Distorted dust caps

- a. Re-time the pinions.
- b. 24 balls only.
- c. Re-adjust both cones.
- d. Adjust as needed. Very important.
- e. Replace all distorted dust caps.

No gear action at all.
- a. Pawls stuck-no oil or bad oil.

- a. Use a free flowing oil.

Sluggish gear change.
- a. Distorted axle spring.
- b. Bent axle.
- c. Worn toggle chain link.
- d. Rusty or frayed cable.

- a. Replace the spring.
- b. Replace the axle.
- c. Replace indicator and chain.
- d. Replace frayed cable.

Safety.

In my home state of Arizona there were 392 reported accidents involving an automobile and a bicycle, during 1969. Five of the bike riders were killed and many were seriously injured. There were an additional 357 instances where a total of 387 persons (75% under 15 years of age) suffered an injury. Many of these accidents involved people riding double.

To quote Harold J. Grieve, Supervisor of Traffic Safety Education department, the Arizona Highway Department, "When a three-thousand-pound-motor vehicle collides with a fifty-pound bicycle the advantage is bound to be on the side of the motor vehicle. This holds true when the cycle runs into the car as well as when the car runs into the cycle."

Mister Grieve continues, "Most bicycles are ridden by youngsters. Partly because riders are not required to wear helmets or protective clothing, they are extremely vulnerable to injury when involved in a collision."

"Young bike riders are often untrained in traffic law and proper procedures. In some cases they are actually mis-trained. There have been a large number of reported instances in which bike riders were wrongfully taught to ride on the left side of the street "so they could face traffic", as is proper only for pedestrians."

In a open letter to parents of Arizona, and this should apply everywhere, Mister Grieve adds that 74% of bike-auto crashes involve children under 15, and in 90% of the cases, the automobile driver was not in violation. The young bike rider must be informed about the law, and good safety habits.

Operation of Bicycles and Play Vehicles-Arizona Law
(Courtesy Traffic Safety Division, Arizona Highway Department, John T. Wood, Superintendent).
Arizona Revised Statutes.
28-811

A. The parent of a child or the guardian of a ward shall not authorize, or knowingly permit the child or ward to violate any of the provisions of this chapter.

B. The regulations of this chapter in their application to bicycles shall apply when a bicycle is operated upon any highway or upon any path set aside for the exclusive use of bicycles subject to those exceptions stated in this article.

28-812

Every person riding a bicycle upon a roadway shall be granted all rights and shall be subject to all the duties applicable to the driver of a vehicle by this chapter, except as to special regulations in this article, and except as to those provisions of this chapter which by their nature can have no application.

28-813 Riding on Bicycles.

A. A person propelling a bicycle shall not ride other than upon or astride a permanent and regular seat attached thereto.

B. No bicycle shall be used to carry more persons at one time than the number for which it is designed or equipped.

28-814 Clinging to vehicles.

No person riding upon any bicycle, coaster, roller skates, sled or toy vehicle shall attach himself or same to any vehicle upon a roadway.

Safety (continued).

28-815 Riding on roadways or bicycle paths.
    A. Every person operating a bicycle upon a roadway shall ride as near the right side of the roadway as practicable, exercising due care when passing a standing vehicle or one proceeding in the same direction.
    B. Persons riding bicycles upon a roadway shall not ride more than two abreast except on paths or parts of roadways set aside for exclusive use of bicycles.
    C. Wherever a usable path for bicycle has been provided adjacent to a roadway, bicycle riders shall use the path and shall not use the roadway.

28-816 Carrying articles.
    No person operating a bicycle shall carry any package, bundle or article which prevents the driver from keeping at least one hand on the handlebars.

28-817 Lamps and other equipment on bicycles.
    A. Every bicycle when in use at nighttime shall be equipped with a lamp on the front which shall emit a white light visible from a distance of at least five hundred feet to the front and with a red reflector on the rear of a type approved by the department which shall be visible from all distances from fifty to three hundred feet to the rear when directly in front of lawful upper beams of head lamps on motor vehicles. A lamp emitting a red light visible from a distance of five hundred feet to the rear may be used in addition to the red reflector.
    B. No person shall operate a bicycle equipped with a siren or whistle.
    C. Every bicycle shall be equipped with a brake which will enable the operator to make the braked wheels skid on dry, level, clean pavement.

25 Safety rules for good bicycle riding.
    1. Ride on the right hand side of roadways, with the traffic.
    2. Ride single file if with a group.
    3. Obey all traffic signals and signs. (see page 87)
    4. When possible, use less traveled roadways.
    5. Never ride on high speed highways (freeways).
    6. Be sure to signal your intentions to turn or stop.
    7. Yield right-of-way to pedestrians and AUTOMOBILES.
    8. Walk your bike across busy streets at the intersection.
    9. Refuse to carry passengers or large packages.
    10. Make all bike repairs off the roadway.
    11. Always stop or park off the paved portion of the highway.
    12. Come to a full stop before entering a street or highway.
    13. Never hitch rides or ride closely behind any vehicle.
    14. Never ride out from between parked cars.
    15. Your bike should be equipped with a white headlight and a red rear reflector for night riding.
    16. Wear light colored clothing when riding at night.
    17. Any bike used frequently after dark should be painted white.
    18. Carry parcels only in an approved rack or carrier.
    19. Equip your bike with a bell or other warning device.
    20. Ride in a straight line-never weave in and out of traffic.
    21. Make left turns from traffic lane nearest center line.
        Make right turns from lane nearest the curb.
    22. Always park your bike in a designated spot, out of any traffic flow.
    23. Avoid riding your bike if you're tired or ill.
    24. Avoid riding in bad or stormy weather.
    25. Your bike is a slow moving vehicle, don't interfere with traffic flow.

Learning to ride in traffic.

When riding in traffic, learn the signs. They might save your life.

Traffic signs The three types of traffic signs are classified according to function. They are regulatory, warning and information or guide signs.

KNOW THESE SIGNS BY THEIR SHAPES.

Signs, and their Shapes

Stop

Yield Right of Way

Speed

Railroad Warning or Evacuation Route

Warning Sign

Highway Markers

Hand signal for left turn.

Hand signal for right turn.

Hand signal for slow or stop.

Warning Signs—Black and Yellow

There is a "Stop" and "Go" traffic light ahead.

You are entering a one-way roadway.

You are leaving a one-way roadway.

PEDESTRIANS
BICYCLES
EQUESTRIANS
MOTOR DRIVEN
CYCLES
UNDER 5 HP
PROHIBITED
ON FREEWAY

Page 88

Acknowledgements:

Bicycle Journal, Fort Worth, Texas
AMF Hercules Division div.
Monark Bicycle Company, Sweden
Japan Bicycle Industry Association
Japan's Bicycle guide, volume 18, 1968
LC Bicycle Service Company
Arizona State Highway Department, Traffic Safety, John T. Wood, Supt.